CASTLES
Scotland & the Border Country

CASTLES
Scotland & the Border Country

THE ESSENTIAL VISITOR GUIDE TO THE BEST OF THE REGION

Based on the classic work by Plantagenet Somerset Fry
Revised and updated by Pip Leahy

A DAVID & CHARLES BOOK

Copyright © David & Charles Limited 2007

David & Charles is an F+W Publications
Inc. company
4700 East Galbraith Road
Cincinnati, OH 45236

First published in the UK in 2007

This book is based on the research undertaken for
Castles, first published in 2005, which in turn was
based on the research undertaken for *Castles of
Britain and Ireland* by Plantagenet Somerset Fry,
last paperback edition published 2001.

A catalogue record for this book is available
from the British Library.

ISBN-13: 978-0-7153-2707-4
ISBN-10: 0-7153-2707-0

Printed in China by SNP Leefung
for David & Charles
Brunel House   Newton Abbot   Devon

Commissioning Editor: Neil Baber
Editor: Emily Pitcher
Project Editor: Ame Verso
Research and Additional Writing: Pip Leahy
Head of Design: Prudence Rogers
Designer: Eleanor Stafford
Production Controller: Ros Napper
Maps: Ethan Danielson

Visit our website at www.davidandcharles.co.uk

David & Charles books are available from all
good bookshops; alternatively you can contact
our Orderline on 0870 9908222 or write to us
at FREEPOST EX2 110, D&C Direct, Newton
Abbot, TQ12 4ZZ (no stamp required UK only);
US customers call 800-289-0963 and Canadian
customers call 800-840-5220.

ACKNOWLEDGMENTS

The publisher is grateful to Matthew Shelley
at Historic Scotland for his advice and help.
The editors acknowledge the work of Marilynne
Lanng on previous editions of this book.

PICTURE CREDITS

All images copyright © David Lyons except:
pp27, 42t, 45, 54, 59 and 67 copyright ©
epicscotland.com; pp25, 34, 42b, 43, 44, 60,
64–5, 70 and 71 copyright © Colin Palmer
www.buyimage.com

DISCLAIMER

The information in this book is correct at the time
of going to press. However, the information is
intended to be used as a guide only and readers
are advised that they should contact the individual
castles to check the information is correct prior to
visiting. The publisher can accept no responsibility
for inaccuracy and any inconvenience caused.

Contents

Using This Book

Defining castles

Castles: Scotland & the Border Country includes descriptions of more than one hundred castles. The definition of the word 'castle' is generally taken to be a fortified military residence. In this respect they are considered to be different to their precursors, hill forts, Roman forts and Saxon burhs, for example. All of these were military establishments but they were not usually also places to live in permanently. However, not all the castles described in this book fit into a neat category; they have been included to provide a fuller picture.

Providing more information

As well as describing the castles as architecture, in most cases background information is provided. Especially interesting castles are given more space. You might find that these castles are out of their true alphabetical order, but you can locate them using the index.

The book has a Key Dates list on pages 8–10, and a series of introductory features on pages 11–21. These include some brief background information on Scottish history, the origins of castles in general, and their specific development in Scotland and the border region. A glossary of architectural terms can be found on page 122.

The castles included

This book focuses mainly on Scottish castles, but as many English border castles are accessible for a day trip from Scotland (i.e. within 80km/50 miles of the border), the best of these have also been included. Durham Castle is also featured, as although it lies further from the boundary, its importance as a border castle cannot be overlooked. For a comprehensive gazetteer of castles see *Castles* (D&C, 2005) from which this book was derived.

Opening times/access information

Opening times and other useful information is included, but please be aware that such information is subject to change, and therefore the publisher cannot accept responsibility if the information provided has changed. In as many cases as possible we have provided telephone numbers and website addresses, and visitors may wish to check details, in particular admission prices, before planning a visit. Full contact information for Historic Scotland, The National Trust and English Heritage is included on page 124.

By their nature, castles often have areas where visitors should exercise caution and the publisher cannot accept responsibility for any accident or event as a result of using this book.

Locations and maps

For ease of use, the castles have been divided into four key geographic areas (see map opposite). If the castle is in the village or town that has the same name, the location information is limited to its county or statutory area. If it is in a very small settlement, or in the countryside, the nearest village or town is named. National grid map references are given for every entry. A map for each area is included at the beginning of each section.

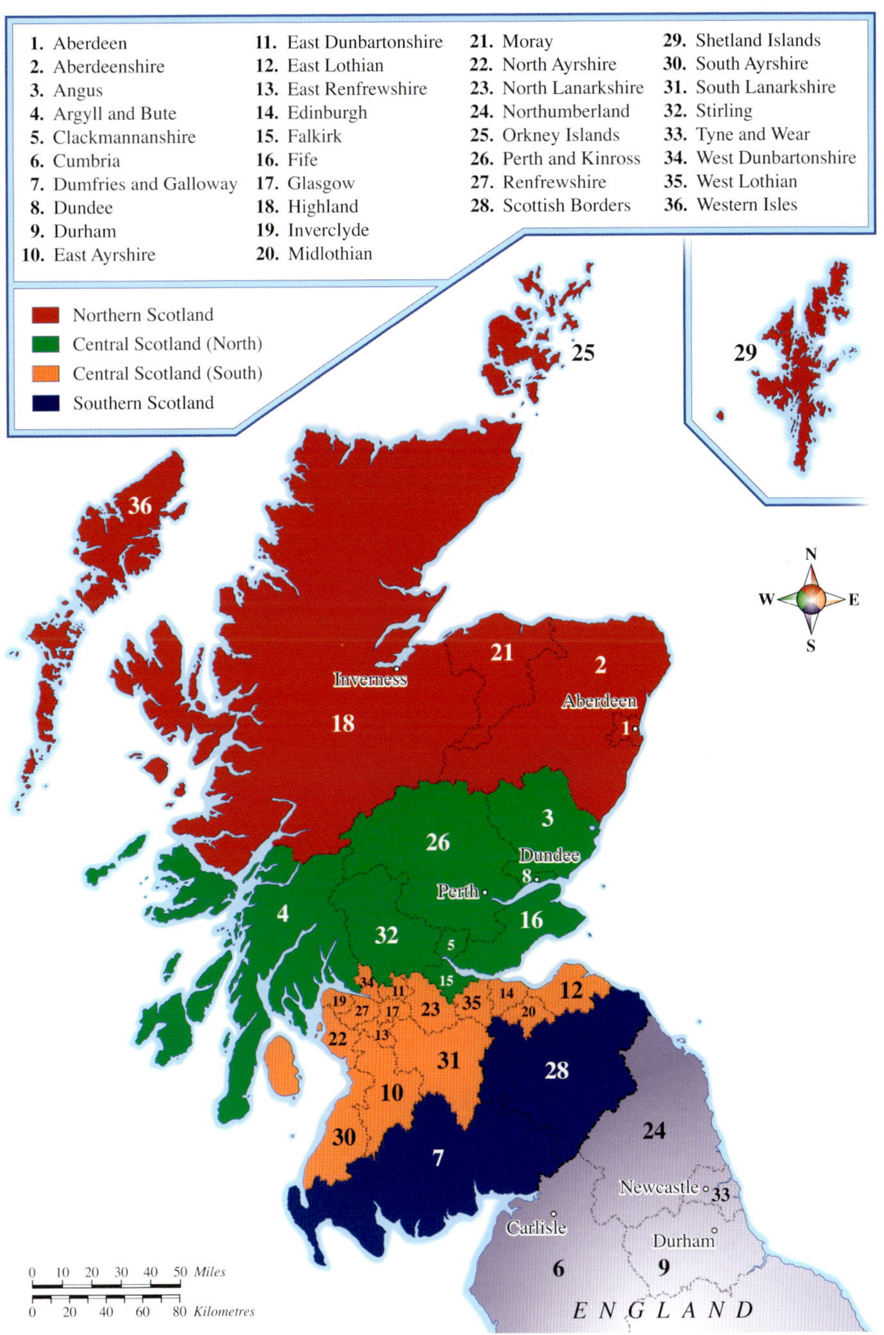

1. Aberdeen
2. Aberdeenshire
3. Angus
4. Argyll and Bute
5. Clackmannanshire
6. Cumbria
7. Dumfries and Galloway
8. Dundee
9. Durham
10. East Ayrshire
11. East Dunbartonshire
12. East Lothian
13. East Renfrewshire
14. Edinburgh
15. Falkirk
16. Fife
17. Glasgow
18. Highland
19. Inverclyde
20. Midlothian
21. Moray
22. North Ayrshire
23. North Lanarkshire
24. Northumberland
25. Orkney Islands
26. Perth and Kinross
27. Renfrewshire
28. Scottish Borders
29. Shetland Islands
30. South Ayrshire
31. South Lanarkshire
32. Stirling
33. Tyne and Wear
34. West Dunbartonshire
35. West Lothian
36. Western Isles
Northern Scotland
Central Scotland (North)
Central Scotland (South)
Southern Scotland
Inverness
Aberdeen
Dundee
Perth
Newcastle
Carlisle
Durham
ENGLAND
N
W E
S
0 10 20 30 40 50 Miles
0 20 40 60 80 Kilometres

Key Dates

Castles are a product both of their times, and of the dominant personalities of their era. By their nature, castles date from times of war, insecurity and danger. As peace and security became the norm, castles were abandoned or adapted for peaceful times. The key events set out below are intended to help put castles into their historical context. Included are dates and events from Scottish and English history, but this is not intended to be a full summary of the history of the two countries.

> **KEY** + England + Scotland + Great Britain

- **43–410** Roman conquest of Britain
- **122** Hadrian's Wall begun
- **793** Vikings attack monastery at Lindisfarne
- **795** Viking raids on Iona
- **843–858 Kenneth McAlpin (Kenneth I)**
- **871–899 Alfred the Great**
- **1034–1040 Duncan I**
- **1040–1057 Macbeth**
- **1042–1066 Edward I** (the Confessor)
- **1057–1058 Lulach**
- **1058–1093 Malcolm III**
- **1066 Harold II**
- **1066** Battle of Stamford Bridge
- **1066** William I (the Conqueror) lands in Britain
- **1066** Battle of Hastings
- **1066–1087 William I**
- **1069–1070** Harrying of the North. Many Northern English lords flee to Scotland
- **1072** Treaty of Abernethy. Malcolm III recognizes William the Conqueror's overlordship
- **1080** Domesday Survey ordered
- **1087–1100 William II**
- **1093** Battle of Alnwick – Malcolm III and his son Edward killed
- **1093–1097 Donald III**
- **1097–1107 Edgar**

- **1100** Malcolm III's daughter marries Henry I of England
- **1100–1135 Henry I**
- **1107–1124 Alexander I**
- **1124–1153 David I**
- **1135–1154 Stephen**
- **1138–1148** Civil war between Stephen and Matilda
- **1138** Scots invade Northumberland
- **1138** Battle of the Standard
- **1141** Stephen captured by Matilda's forces at Battle of Lincoln. Matilda elected Queen of England. Stephen released later in year
- **1153–1165 Malcolm IV**
- **1154–1189 Henry II**
- **1165–1214 William I**
- **1174** Battle of Alnwick. William I invades northern England in support of barons' rebellion against Henry II. William captured and forced to accept Henry II as superior in the Treaty of Falaise
- **1189–1199 Richard I** (the Lionheart)
- **1199–1216 John**
- **1214–1216** Barons' Revolt
- **1214–1249 Alexander II**
- **1215** Magna Carta
- **1216–1272 Henry III**

- **1237** Scottish border with England fixed at the point where it has more or less remained ever since
- **1249–1286 Alexander III**
- **1252** Henry III's daughter marries Alexander III of Scotland
- **1264–1267** Barons' War
- **1266** Hebrides and Isle of Man given to Scots by King of Norway
- **1272–1307 Edward I**
- **1277** Edward I begins his war on Wales
- **1286–1290 Margaret**
- **1290–1292 First Interregnum**
- **1292–1296 John Balliol**
- **1295** The Auld Alliance
- **1295–1363** Scottish Wars of Independence
- **1296** Battle of Dunbar (between Balliol and Edward I)
- **1297** Battle of Stirling Bridge
- **1298** Battle of Falkirk – Wallace defeated
- **1296–1306** Second Interregnum
- **1306–1329 Robert I** (the Bruce)
- **1307** Battle of Loudoun Hill
- **1307–1327 Edward II**
- **1312** Piers Gaveston executed
- **1314** Battle of Bannockburn
- **1320** Declaration of Arbroath – Scottish Independence
- **1327–1377 Edward III**
- **1329–1371 David II**
- **1337–1453** Hundred Years' War
- **1346** Battle of Neville's Cross. David II imprisoned for 11 years
- **1371–1390 Robert II**
- **1377–1399 Richard II**
- **1384** French army lands to help Scots attack the north of England
- **1390–1406 Robert III**
- **1399** Richard II imprisoned at Pontefract Castle

- **1399–1413 Henry IV**
- **1403–1409** Percys' Revolt
- **1406–1437 James I**
- **1408** Battle of Bramham Moor. Death of Henry Percy, Earl of Northumberland
- **1410** Founding of St Andrews University
- **1413–1422 Henry V**
- **1422–1461 Henry VI**
- **1437–1460 James II**
- **1453–1485** Wars of the Roses
- **1460–1488 James III**
- **1461–1470 Edward IV**
- **1470–1471 Henry VI**
- **1471** Battle of Barnet: death of Richard Neville, Earl of Warwick
- **1471** Battle of Tewkesbury: death of Edward, Prince of Wales
- **1471–1483 Edward IV**
- **1483 Edward V** – one of the princes allegedly murdered in the Tower of London
- **1483–1485 Richard III**
- **1485** Battle of Bosworth Field
- **1485–1509 Henry VII**
- **1488** Battle of Sauchieburn
- **1488–1513 James IV**
- **1503** James IV marries Henry VII's daughter, Margaret Tudor
- **1509–1547 Henry VIII**
- **1513–1542 James V**
- **1513** Battle of Flodden Field
- **1534** Act of Supremacy
- **1536–1540** Dissolution of the Monasteries
- **1536** Pilgrimage of Grace
- **1542–1567 Mary, Queen of Scots**
- **1542** Battle of Solway Moss
- **1543–1548** Rough Wooing
- **1547–1553 Edward VI**
- **1547** Battle of Pinkie

- **1553–1558 Mary I**
- **1554** Mary marries Philip of Spain
- **1558–1603 Elizabeth I**
- **1560** Treaty of Edinburgh – the end of the Auld Alliance and withdrawal of French troops from Scotland
- **1567** Mary, Queen of Scots is held prisoner at Lochleven Castle where she is forced to abdicate in favour of her son
- **1567–1625 James VI**
- **1567–1573** Scottish Civil War
- **1569** Rising of the North
- **1573** Fall of Edinburgh Castle
- **1587** Execution of Mary, Queen of Scots at Fotheringhay Castle
- **1588** Spanish Armada
- **1603–1625 James I** (Union of the Crowns of Scotland and England; end of the war with Spain)
- **1605** Gunpowder Plot
- **1625–1649 Charles I**
- **1642–1646** English Civil War
- **1648–1651** English Civil War
- **1649–1660** The Commonwealth
- **1649–1685 Charles II**
- **1660** Restoration of the Monarchy
- **1660–1685 Charles II**

- **1685–1688 James II** (VII of Scotland)
- **1688** Glorious Revolution
- **1689–1745** Jacobite Uprisings
- **1689–1702 William III & Mary**
- **1689–1694 Mary II**
- **1702–1714 Anne**
- **1707** Act of Union with Scotland
- **1714–1727 George I**
- **1727–1760 George II**
- **1746** Battle of Culloden Moor – last military battle on British soil
- **1746** Blair Castle besieged – last siege of a castle in Britain
- **1760–1820 George III**
- **1803–1815** Napoleonic Wars
- **1820–1830 George IV**
- **1830–1837 William IV**
- **1837–1901 Victoria**
- **1901–1910 Edward VII**
- **1910–1936 George V**
- **1914–1918** World War I
- **1936** Abdication of Edward VIII
- **1936–1952 George VI**
- **1939–1945** World War II – last active use of castles on British soil
- **1952–present Elizabeth II**
- **1998** Current Scottish Parliament established by the Scotland Act

Scotland: A Brief History

The Romans and Anglo-Saxons

Although Roman invaders made attempts to conquer the inhospitable northern territories, they never succeeded in subjugating the tribal kingdoms of Scotland. In AD122 the Emperor Hadrian built his immense defensive wall between the Solway Firth in the west and the Tyne in the east. Around two decades later a new frontier was established between the Clyde and the Forth, guarded by the Antonine Wall, but this was abandoned about 20 years later.

Early in the 5th century the Romans left Britannia and the conquest of England by the Anglo-Saxons began. Like the Romans, the Germanic Anglo-Saxons never truly wielded their influence in the northern territories. By the 6th century there were three main peoples inhabiting the north – the Dalriadans (or Scotti) who were Irish Gaels, the Picts and the Britons, who had been pushed north (and west) by the Anglo-Saxons.

The Vikings

The first recorded attack on Scotland by Scandinavian Vikings was on the island of Iona in 795. Large-scale settlements of Norwegian Vikings on the Northern Isles (Shetland and Orkney) began around 800; the Western Isles and northern Scottish mainland had Viking settlements around 50 years later. A monumental victory for Viking forces in 839 virtually eliminated the Pictish and Dalriadan 'aristocracy': it was after this that Kenneth McAlpin (Kenneth I) joined the two territories to create one kingdom known as Alba, of which he was King. His grandson Donald II was the first ruler to use the title King of Scotland.

The Normans

William the Conqueror never succeeded in occupying the Scottish territories, however Scotland's Malcolm III became William's vassal under the Treaty of Abernethy in 1072. When Malcolm III came to the throne in 1058 most Scots spoke Gaelic and the Celtic Church was dominant. Malcolm's wife, Margaret, an Anglo-Saxon princess, did much to Anglicize the Scottish court but it was their son David I, who had grown up at the court of Henry I of England, who brought Anglo-Norman families (luring them with land in return for their support), Norman culture and customs, including feudalism, to the kingdom. Within a few generations Anglo-Normans were integrated into Scottish society. David also founded great monasteries: these were not only religious centres but cultural and economic powerhouses.

Although it seems unlikely now, this rocky outcrop was once one of the most important places in Scotland. Dunnadd was the capital of the kingdom of Dalriada, founded by incoming Irish tribespeople known as Scotti.

The Wars of Independence

The House of McAlpin continued to rule Scotland until the latter half of the 13th century when the last of the McAlpin rulers, Alexander III, ruled over a kingdom equating to modern Scotland (with the exception of Orkney and Shetland which were still under the control of the Norwegians). When Alexander died in 1286 his only heir was his infant granddaughter Margaret, daughter of King Eric of Norway. Margaret died on the journey from Norway to Scotland, provoking a crisis over the succession, which would lead to the Scottish Wars of Independence and the Scottish alliance with the French (the Auld Alliance), which would last until the Reformation.

The Wars of Independence were essentially a series of military campaigns against English supremacy, which raged until the middle of the 14th century. The first of these was instigated by Edward I's invasion of Scotland in 1296 and saw the rise of two legendary figures in Scottish history, William Wallace and Robert Bruce. Scottish independence was declared under the Treaty of Arbroath in 1320 but the struggles with England were to continue. During the second War of Independence, Bruce's son David II, was held prisoner by the English for 11 years after his defeat at Neville's Cross. He was released in 1357 only after the payment of a sizeable ransom but most importantly Scotland had remained free from English rule.

The Stewart monarchs

The House of Stewart began when David's nephew Robert II succeeded him; he was the first in a line of Stewart monarchs that would rule Scotland for more than three centuries. One of the most famous was the romantic and tragic figure of the Catholic Mary, Queen of Scots whose turbulent life was ended by the Protestant English Queen Elizabeth I in 1586. Mary was mother to James VI, the King who would unite the Scottish and English crowns and become James I of England.

The Civil War

The Scottish uprising against the religious policies of Charles I sparked the Civil War in England. Scotland's protestors formed a group known as the Covenanters at the end of the 1630s. The unrest about Charles soon spread, first to Ireland and then in 1642, the English Civil War broke out. Initially the Covenanters allied themselves with the English Parliament against the King but then switched allegiance and rallied to the cause of the exiled Charles II, causing Cromwell's forces to invade in 1650. The fortress of Dunnottar was the last Royalist

Kildrummy Castle's strategic location commanded important routes across northern Scotland. The castle served as a base for the Earl of Mar when he raised the standard to launch the 1715 Jacobite Uprising.

stronghold to hold out against the English Parliamentarian forces, but it fell in 1652 and the kingdom was under occupation until the Restoration of Charles II in 1660.

The Jacobite Uprisings

Charles's brother James II (James VII of Scotland) came to the throne in 1685. His Catholic sympathies and belief in the Divine Right of Kings paved the way for his protestant son-in-law, William of Orange, to carry out the only successful invasion of England since the Norman conquest. He ruled with his wife Mary, James II's daughter, after James was deposed in 1688, and it was during his reign in 1692 that the infamous massacre of Glencoe took place, when the MacDonalds were killed by the Campbells, on Government orders, after they delayed making an oath of allegiance to William. In the 60 years that followed the accession of William and Mary there were numerous attempts to restore James and his descendents to the throne, supported by Catholic Spain and France. Two key figures in these attempted coups were James Edward Stuart known as 'The Old Pretender' and his son Charles Edward Stuart or 'Bonnie Prince Charlie' (James II's son and grandson). The final clash between the Jacobites and the Royal House of Hanover came at Culloden Moor in April 1746. The Jacobite defeat led to 'Bonnie Prince Charlie' fleeing to exile in France, the dismantling of the clan system and removing the power of the clan chiefs.

Union

Meanwhile, in 1707 the Treaty of Union between England and Scotland was ratified and the first Parliament of Great Britain met in London.

During the Civil War Blair Castle was a Royalist stronghold and a prime target for Cromwell's troops – they captured it in 1652 and held it for eight years, until Charles II was restored to the throne.

The Development of Castles

Early fortresses

The idea of castles grew out of the fortifications that men had used for centuries. Some of the most conspicuous of these are the great hill forts built in the Iron Age, which consisted of enormous earthen ramparts, originally topped by wooden walls and walkways, and surrounded by deep ditches such as Danebury in Hampshire, Traprain Law in East Lothian and Dunnadd in Argyll and Bute. These forts were at the core of highly organized and sophisticated tribal societies. Scotland, which was continually threatened by Viking incursions and tribal conflict, also had its Crannogs (artificial islands) and the small, fortified towers known as Brochs to serve as protection against invaders.

Norman castles

It was the Normans who introduced the fortresses that we know as castles. Based on structures in use on the European mainland since at least the 9th century, within a short time of the invasion, Norman castles were built all over the British Isles – they were to become the symbol of Norman might and conquest. The Normans built their wooden motte-and-bailey castles to help conquer in purely military terms, but the stone castles that followed were intended to dominate in psychological ways as well. Nothing like these immense stone structures had been seen in Britain before.

Feudalism

Castles were central to the feudal system – they belonged to the lords or barons who built them. Scotland's Kings adopted the feudal system of landholding in the 12th century and lands were granted to loyal supporters of the crown. In the Highlands and the North, where Celtic princes held power (with only nominal loyalty to the King) baronies were granted by the local rulers. Land and other benefits were granted in return for the barons' fealty and service. These lords and barons built castles – for defence, to regroup in, to hold provisions in, and to rule from – and castles were also home to their families and close retainers. As the first wooden castles were replaced by more permanent and secure structures of stone, so there were opportunities to introduce some degree of comfort and architectural improvements.

Castle Donan is the traditional home of the MacRae Clan. Originally built in the 13th century, it was left in ruins after bombardment by warships in 1719. It was restored in the first half of the 20th century.

A vital role

Castles and tower houses played a vital role in medieval history. They were the strong place from which attacks and rebellions were begun, and they were the refuges that offered protection when needed. These fortress residences were built and destroyed often, and many were already in ruins in medieval times. Sometimes they remained ruinous because their strategic value had diminished, or sometimes it was because their owners and their families could not afford to repair them, or were dead.

At Dunnottar Castle, which sits on a promontory jutting out into the North Sea, the wall nearest the mainland was equipped with gun ports, despite its conversion to a palatial residence in the late 16th century.

Strongholds in disputed regions were particularly vulnerable, and it was in these areas that there were most castles. Like Wales and Ireland, Scotland's rugged and wild landscapes aided its native warriors, who could behave like guerrilla fighters and disappear into the mountain fastnesses when they wanted to. But their castles and tower houses played a key role: they guarded the important towns, ports and passes, and some became the strongholds of the Scottish clans. Scottish leaders sought help from many quarters in their struggles with the English, often bringing soldiers in from elsewhere in Europe and with them came new, Continental ideas of castle design.

Perhaps the most impressive single group of castles in the British Isles is Edward I's 'Ring of Iron' in North Wales. Once Edward had subjugated Wales he turned his attention to Scotland.

The decline of castles

Castles gradually ceased to have a defensive role throughout much of the British Isles, though internecine struggles and the English threat kept Scottish fortresses in a defensive role for far longer. Castles all over the British Isles came into their own again during the Civil War of the 17th century – many were destroyed in sieges and many more were slighted so they could not be used again. Dunnottar was the last Scottish stronghold to fall to the English Parliament's troops, a mighty fortress that never fully recovered from Cromwell's bombardment.

Castles in Scotland

The basic plan of most Norman castles is the same, with the motte (mound) at the centre of the defences. Greater variety followed when stone defences and buildings were added. Here at Duffus Castle the stone tower is linked to the outer defences of the bailey by a great curtain wall.

Early Scottish castles

Scottish castles were introduced, not by force as they were in England and Wales, but by choice, by Scottish Kings who were influenced by Norman ideas, and by Norman Lords whom the Kings welcomed into Scotland and to whom they gave lands (in many cases with permission to build castles). The Kings were, in effect, implementing the introduction of feudalism into parts of Scotland, mostly into the Lowlands and the north-east of the country.

The first castles in Scotland therefore were mainly motte castles, and between about 1100 and 1250 more than 200 were raised. Duffus is a prime example. These castles were constructed in the same way as English motte castles and played much the same role, for while the Kings of Scotland and their lords were 'feudalists', their subjects were not so receptive to the new order. Scottish castles had additional roles: to act as fortresses for the defence of the country against attack from England, and also against continued Viking incursions up to the middle of the 13th century. Motte castles were raised in south-west Scotland in some quantity; they were also built north of the Forth in a north-easterly sweep.

Stone fortresses

Some of the earliest stone castles in Scotland were built by the Norse – Cubbie Roo's on the Isle of Orkney, for example. As in England and Wales, Scottish stone castles began to be built alongside the earthwork-and-timber motte castles. These stone fortresses emerged in the main patterns familiar elsewhere – the great tower (or keep) and a curtain enclosure or barmkin, with flanking towers and other buildings inside: Kisimul is an enduring example.

Many more of these simpler enclosure castles were built in the 12th and 13th centuries. But more elaborate enclosures, dating to the 13th century, include Kildrummy and Dirleton. Shell enclosures were rare but the best known of these is Rothesay in Argyll and Bute.

The tower house

The 14th century saw the emergence of the Scottish tower house, which was to become the standard style of lordly residence in the land for several centuries and completely dominated Scottish castle building. Probably around 700 of these tall fortified residences were constructed in every part of the country. The first tower houses were extremely well put together – the survival of so many of them is testimony to the strength of their construction. By the end of the 14th century, the need for fortified residences, diminishing in England and Wales, was more pressing than ever in Scotland despite the end of the Wars of Independence. The English threat was still ever-present and the clan chiefs continued to menace the kingdom's stability and order.

From basic beginnings

Early tower houses provided a very basic form of accommodation: most of the 14th- and 15th-century tower houses were not large and nothing like the size of the 12th-century English keeps, but by the 15th and 16th centuries the need for more comfortable living meant that in many cases they became almost palatial, yet without losing their defensibility. Numerous tower houses were given walls many feet thick, about three times the average thickness of house walls today. The towers had battlemented parapets (like Drum for example) or parapets protected by toughened corbelled turrets on the corners overlooking them, or both.

Defensive measures

Tower houses were also surrounded by ditches and banks, the moats sometimes being fed by nearby streams or rivers, with drawbridges across them leading to and from gateways. Frequently, tall stone curtains, which in Scotland are often known as barmkins, surrounded

the towers. Most of the early tower houses had the entrance on the first floor, reached by a stone or wooden stairway, or even a simple ladder. Their basements would have had

Dirleton Castle began as an earth-and-timber construction built by the Norman de Vaux family who were encouraged to settle in Scotland by David I in the 12th century. The castle was added to over the following centuries to become an elaborate range of buildings.

no access to the first floor except by a single hatch in the ceiling. Most of these first-floor entrances were protected by an iron yett, an openwork grille of interlacing iron bars that acted like a portcullis. Some could be raised and lowered, other swung open and shut on hinges. Sometimes chambers with spy-holes were built into the wall thicknesses – these were a medieval form of 'bugging' and were known as luggies. There is a luggie at Castle Fraser.

From the last decades of the 15th century onwards a few tower houses began to be equipped with gun-ports for small cannons and other artillery. The cannon was not regarded as a major war weapon until the 16th century, by which time a variety of small guns, including handguns, had come into use. This was reflected by the appearance of small gun-ports in a variety of styles in numerous castles. Ravenscraig was the first castle in Britain to be designed for systematic defence by guns.

Caerlaverock Castle, built by the Maxwell family, enjoyed peaceful prosperity until 1300 when Lord Maxwell's garrison became a target for Edward I's wrath against Scots resistance and was forced to surrender to the might of the besieging army.

Troubled times

Military uses of the English and Welsh castles (aside from the fortresses in the English border counties) came to an end early in the 16th century, although their role was revived in the Civil War of the 17th century. Scotland though needed its fortresses more than ever – the gradual weakening of the Auld Alliance with France coincided with growing aggression from the English – the period included the notorious 'rough wooing' of 1543–8 when Edinburgh was burnt. Three times in a century the kingdom had passed from a dead or deposed monarch to an infant successor. Years of minority rule, when one faction after another jockeyed, intrigued and even murdered to gain power recreated the sort of anarchy England had seen during Stephen's reign in the first half of the 12th century. This uncertain atmosphere saw lords fortifying their castles and attacking those of their rivals. While the leading men, lesser lairds and rich merchants of Scotland chose to shut themselves in strong, tall, ill-lit fortresses of stone, their contemporaries in England were building horizontal residences of brick with tall, wide windows without a gun-port to be seen. Building activity slowed in the decades after the Battle of Flodden Field in 1513 – a fresh impetus was experienced with the troubles of the time of Mary, Queen of Scots.

Stairways

Considerable attention was given to staircases in Scottish tower houses and many were constructed with some ingenuity. The earlier towers had spirals in one corner of the wall thickness, although some had straight mural flights. They were not designed for easy use of the owner but to deter intruders – the flights did not always go up the same corner, which meant that you had to cross the floor to reach another flight, as in some English keeps. In some castles flights crossed over other flights and in others, spiral flights led from the ground to the parapet without opening into intervening floors (which were reached by a second set of stairs). Some tower houses had straight flights as well as spirals and some had false storeys and unexpected changes of floor levels – all designed to baffle unwanted guests.

A development

The desire for more residential space and comfort (kitchens, servants' rooms, guest rooms and so forth) was met with similar attention and ingenuity of design. Plain rectangular tower houses like Crichton and Drum were well provided with chambers, closets and stairs within the wall thicknesses. Before the end of the 14th century the first rectangular tower houses with extending wings had been built, erected as one unit. These were the L-plan tower houses, which were a rectangular tower house block with one short wing (usually square) projecting from one side. Their purpose was to incorporate private apartments and stairs that could be separate from the main block (which usually consisted of one main large hall, that may have been screened off at one end). The wing also enabled the tower to have a well-protected entrance on the ground floor, in the angle of the L, which could be defended by covering fire from both the main block and wing. Later, many of these L-plan towers had gun-ports inserted next to the entrance.

Different styles

The 16th century witnessed new shapes of tower house: the stepped L-plan, the Z-plan and the rectangular tower with various wings added to its sides. The stepped L-plan was an L-plan with an additional square (or occasionally semi-circular) wing in the angle of the L (or re-entrant), which contained the entrance and staircase, as at Craigevar: at Greenknowe Tower the step was a semi-circular turret. The tower with wings added haphazardly round the sides varied individually every time. Elcho has a square tower on the south-west corner, a smaller square tower on the north-west corner and a circular tower on the north-east corner, with a fourth tower, circular with staircase, on the north wall. McLellans has two steps in the re-entrant and a square tower positioned on the south-west corner with separate spiral staircase.

The Z-plan tower house

The first of the Z-plan tower houses were built late in the 15th century (although the period usually associated with them is the second half of the 16th and early years of the 17th centuries). This was a unique style of fortified residence. A rectangular tower block was augmented with two wing towers at diagonally opposite ends of the block. Each wing, equipped with gun-ports and/or shot-holes, covered two faces of the block which in turn, similarly equipped, could cover the wings so that it was impossible to attack the tower house from any direction without coming into the field of fire. The wing towers were square (as at Noltland and Glenbuchat) or circular (as at Claypotts) or even one of each (Tolquhon was a modified Z-plan). Over 60 Z-plan tower houses were built in Scotland.

The 17th century and later

Tower houses continued to be built into the 17th century (as at Craigevar). However, magnificent looking mansions, often built around earlier medieval towers, were becoming more usual – some of these developed into palatial stately homes for Scottish aristocrats, or later still became grand baronial homes in the Victorian Romantic style. Many Scottish castles are still lived in by descendants of the clan chiefs and Kings that played a part in the complicated history of the land. Some lay forlorn and neglected having been abandoned or slighted, but add a picturesque silhouette to a splendid view, and others are for us to share, opened up as visitor attractions or luxurious hotels and holiday accommodation.

Two famous castles

The two most famous castles in Scotland are Edinburgh and Stirling. Both stand on mighty basalt rock mounds dominating the countryside around them and each visible from the other on a clear day. Their strategic positions speak for themselves. Stirling in particular guards the principal routes into the Highlands. Neither of them falls into any of the castle types outlined in these pages. They are royal palace-fortresses, developed over centuries and have both always played a pivotal role in the country's history.

Towers have always been at the heart of castle design, and tower castles and houses were built in very large numbers in Ireland and Scotland. Scotland's Castle Stalker has the added protection of being built on an island, and has mainly been reached by boat. It originally belonged to the Stewart clan, but passed to the Campbells in the 17th century. Descendants of the original Stewart owners regained it at the beginning of the 20th century.

Border Castles

If the need for castles began to diminish generally in England and Wales in the 14th century, there was one area where, on the contrary, it grew. That was the border between England and Scotland, which was for centuries, after the Scots won their War of Independence under Robert Bruce, the scene of warfare, looting and destruction of crops, farms and houses by raiders on both sides. It was also the scene for many better-organized invasions, counter-invasions and 'punitive' expeditions employing armies, siege engines and the other paraphernalia of medieval warfare.

There were great castles and smaller fortified tower houses known as peles. In Northumberland, whose northern boundaries make up about three-quarters of the whole border with Scotland, there are more than 200 of them. Peles probably began as wooden towers, like motte castles and many were built on the remains of older castles, including mottes.

Peles were diminutive, and only effective against the small-scale though tiresome raiding carried out by the Scots. Watching over these smaller castles were the great castles of Alnwick, Bamburgh, Carlisle, Durham, Norham, Newcastle, Prudhoe and Warkworth. Owned and improved by the Crown or by powerful magnates like the Percys, they were among the greatest fortresses in the land, and have had tempestuous histories involving countless sieges and slightings, particularly Carlisle and Norham.

Carlisle Castle has been the site of many sieges by Scottish Kings, including David I, William I, Alexander II, Robert Bruce, and during the Civil War by Leslie, the Scottish general and ally of the Parliamentary cause.

Norham Castle was besieged by Alexander II for six weeks but without success. Robert Bruce tried to take it by siege three times, until a final attempt was successful. It was returned to England under the ensuing peace treaty.

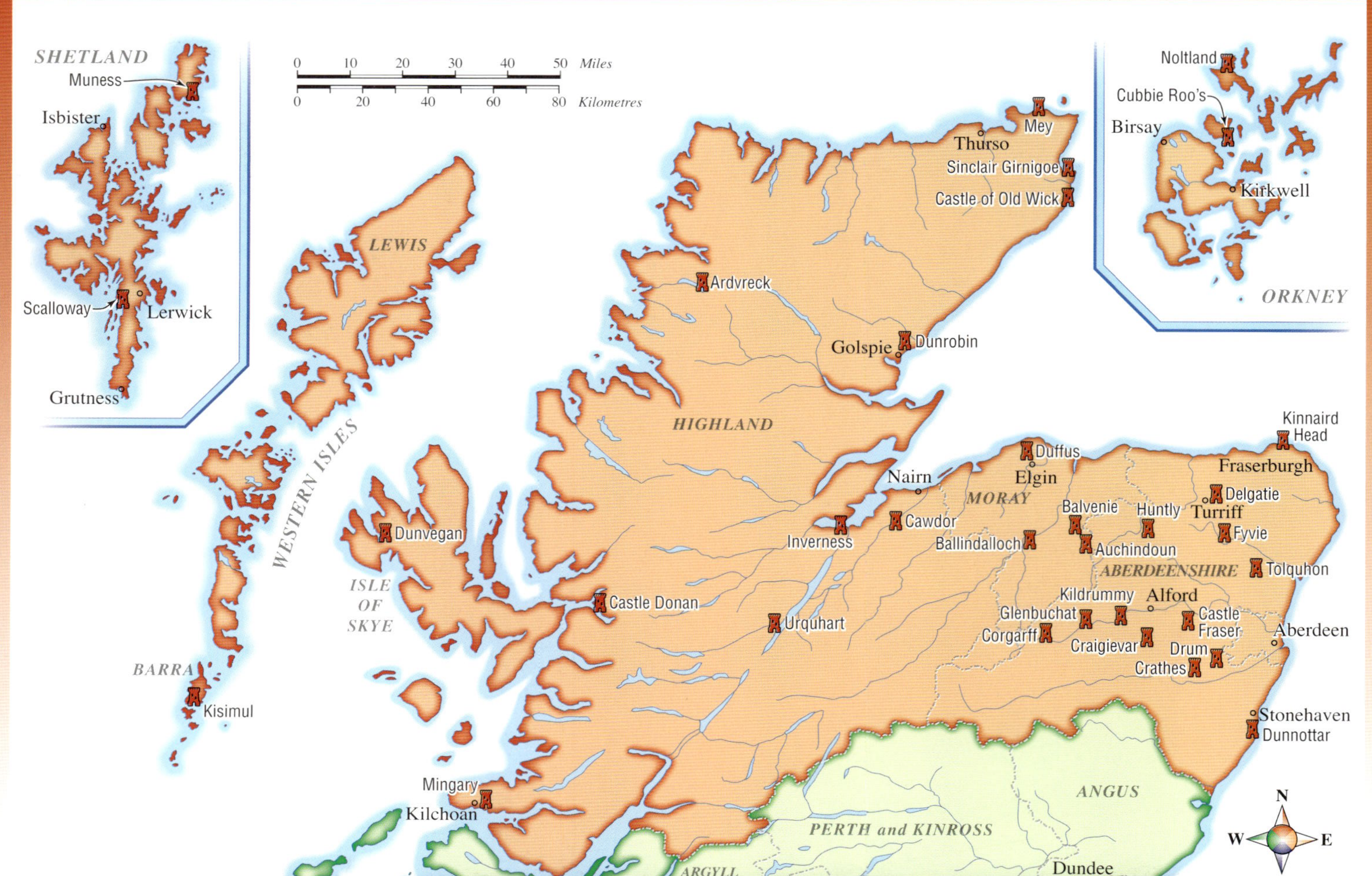

SHETLAND
Muness
Isbister
Scalloway
Lerwick
Grutness
0 10 20 30 40 50 Miles
0 20 40 60 80 Kilometres
Noltland
Cubbie Roo's
Birsay
Kirkwell
ORKNEY
LEWIS
Ardvreck
Mey
Thurso
Sinclair Girnigoe
Castle of Old Wick
Golspie
Dunrobin
HIGHLAND
WESTERN ISLES
Kinnaird Head
Duffus
Fraserburgh
Nairn
Elgin
MORAY
Delgatie
Turriff
Balvenie
Huntly
Dunvegan
Cawdor
Ballindalloch
Auchindoun
Fyvie
ABERDEENSHIRE
Tolquhon
ISLE OF SKYE
Inverness
Kildrummy
Alford
Castle Donan
Glenbuchat
Corgarff
Craigievar
Castle Fraser
Aberdeen
Urquhart
Drum
BARRA
Crathes
Kisimul
Stonehaven
Dunnottar
Mingary
Kilchoan
ANGUS
PERTH and KINROSS
ARGYLL
Dundee
N
E
S
W

Northern Scotland

The far north of Scotland encompasses the Viking strongholds of the Islands of Orkney, Shetland and the Western Isles and includes the iconic castles of Eilean Donan and Cawdor. The Highlands were the sanctuary of Scotland's Celtic heritage and Clan Chiefs held authority here until the 18th century. Norsemen, Normans, Flemish and Celtic overlords established themselves as rulers and fought for territory – leaving a legacy of castles in their wake.

Ardvreck

Perched on a rocky promontory jutting into the
north side of Loch Assynt, Ardvreck is now a
picturesque ruin. It was built in the 16th century
as a simple rectangular tower with a cylindrical
staircase turret at the south-east corner, corbelled out
on the upper storeys. The three chambers on the ground floor were vaulted. After
his defeat at Invercharron in 1650, the Marquis of Montrose, took refuge at Ardvreck,
but was betrayed and handed over to Parliament, which hanged him in Edinburgh.

   The castle was sacked in the 17th century. Although the ruin is too dangerous
to explore, strolling through the captivating scenery of the surrounding countryside
is highly enjoyable.

Location: *Near Inchnadamph, Highland*

Map ref: *NC 239236*

Tel: *01383 860519*

Web: *www.historic-scotland.gov.uk*

Open: *Open access to exterior only*

Auchindoun

Auchindoun was a late 15th-century L-plan tower house
built inside the earthworks of an Iron-Age hill fort. It
was built by Thomas Cochrane, a favourite of James III
who was also responsible for the Great Hall at Stirling
Castle (page 74). The castle was sacked in 1591 by the
Mackintoshes but later restored. It was nevertheless in
ruins by the middle of the 18th century, although there
are still some fine architectural details and the site offers
dramatic views over the surrounding hills.

   Access to the castle is steep and only on foot. Only
the exterior can be seen. Auchindoun is a nice spot for
a picnic if the weather is good.

Location: *Montlach, near Dufftown, Moray*

Map ref: *NJ 348376*

Tel: *01667 460232*

Web: *www.historic-scotland.gov.uk*

Open: *Open access to exterior only*

Ballindalloch

Ballindalloch perfectly illustrates the Scottish architectural transition from fortified tower to more comfortable and charming accommodation. A Z-plan tower house begun in the mid-16th century, Ballindalloch has been enlarged and modified by subsequent generations of the same family to create a building that is known today as the 'Pearl of the North'. One of its most notable inhabitants was the 18th-century bon viveur, General James Grant who added an entire wing to the castle for the sole purpose of housing his favourite French chef.

Location: *Moray*

Map ref: *NJ 179365*

Tel: *01807 500205*

Web: *www.ballindallochcastle.co.uk*

Open: *Sun–Fri 10.30am–5pm (last entry 4.45pm) Easter–end of Sep*

A family home

Ballindalloch's particular attraction is that it is primarily a much-loved family home, filled with memorabilia of the Macpherson-Grants, who have lived at the castle since it was first built. A tour of Ballindalloch takes visitors through interiors where past and present sit comfortably together and which reveal a fine collection of 17th-century Spanish paintings.

Children and adults alike are fascinated by the collection displayed in the castle's nursery, which includes 19th-century teddies and a Georgian high chair. Outside, there is the opportunity to enjoy the lovely gardens and extensive grounds surrounding the castle, which include stretches of the Rivers Spey and Avon, and a 9-hole championship golf course (details are given on the castle website). There is also a well-stocked shop and tearoom.

Location: *Dufftown, Moray*

Map ref: *NJ 326408*

Tel: *01340 820121*

Web: *www.historic-scotland.gov.uk*

Open: *Daily 9.30am–6.30pm Apr–Sep*

Balvenie

Balvenie was built by the Earls of Buchan in the 13th century. The castle once belonged to the 'Black Douglases' but by the middle of the 16th century, it was owned by John Stewart, 4th Earl of Atholl, who completely remodelled the eastern part by constructing a palatial three-storey range with a cylindrical tower, which once had a 'pepper-pot' roof. The castle, occupied until the 18th century, changed hands many times. Its last owner was William Duff.

For the visitor

Balvenie prides itself on offering an accurate insight into life in the keep several hundred years ago. Visitors will particularly enjoy the views from the top of the castle, showing the entrance to the buildings and the moat surrounding them, and into the woods.

Castle Fraser

This is a rectangular tower castle first built in the 15th century. In the late 16th century it was converted to Z-plan and in the 17th century it was enlarged under the supervision of John Bell, a noted mason.

The diagonally opposing four-floor towers are equipped with ornamented shot-holes. There is also a luggie between the vaulting of the hall and the chamber above, which was formed in the thickness of the wall and reached from behind a window shutter. An eavesdropper could slip into the cubicle and listen to goings-on in the hall. The Cowdray family restored the castle early in the 20th century.

Location: *Kemnay, Aberdeenshire*

Map ref: *NJ 722125*

Tel: *01330 833463*

Web: *www.nts.org.uk*

Open: *Daily 11am–5.30pm Jul–Aug; Fri–Tue 12pm–5.30pm Apr–Jun & Sep*

Plenty to see and do

The round tower offers stunning views across the estate. The rooms are richly furnished with 19th-century carpets, curtains and portraits. You can see the Great Hall, the Victorian kitchen, secret stairs and more.

The Woodland Secrets area is an ideal space for children to play safely among sculptures, bamboo figures and a stone circle. The 18th-century walled garden is under renovation and there is an organic vegetable garden, which sometimes supplies ingredients for soups cooked in the Victorian kitchen. A tearoom provides refreshments.

Castle Sinclair Girnigoe

The seat of the Earldom of Caithness used to be known as Castle Girnigoe until early in the 17th century when George Sinclair, the 4th Earl received approval from Parliament to change the name to Castle Sinclair. Notwithstanding this, confusion started as to what its name was, and as a result whether there were one or two castles. Recent archaeological research has shown it was always one castle but as the two names have remained in existence for 400 years it is now known as Castle Sinclair Girnigoe. There were many phases of redevelopment for both military and social reasons, the first dating from the mid to late 14th century and continuing through to the mid-17th century. The castle was the major stronghold in the north of Scotland for Cromwellian troops and it is highly probable that they partially destroyed a lot of the outer bailey to render it uninhabitable in 1660. It has been a ruin ever since. It is still listed as the official seat of the Earls of Caithness and is owned and maintained by the Clan Sinclair Trust, which is working to preserve this spectacular ruin.

Location: *Noss Head, Wick, Highland*

Map ref: *ND 379549*

Tel: *None*

Web: *www.sinclairgirnigoe.org*

Open: *Viewing from the access road at any reasonable time. Please see the website for further information*

Access to the castle

At present access is limited due to ongoing preservation work but there is a good view of the castle from the new access road, where there are also interpretive panels. Part of the castle will be open to the public in the summer of 2007 and more will be opened in phases as and when the preservation work is completed. From the car park at Noss Head the castle is a level 0.8km (½-mile) walk through a breeding area for ground nesting birds (dogs must be kept on leads). The site will be suitable for wheelchair users when the work has been completed.

Location: *Dornie, Highland*

Map ref: *NG 881258*

Tel: *01599 555202*

Web: *www.eileandonancastle.com*

Open: *Daily 10am–5.30pm Apr–Oct;* **Gift Shop:** *open all year*

Castle Donan

This iconic Scottish castle stands on an islet in the Kyle of Lochalsh at the meeting point of three sea lochs, and since 1932 has been joined to the mainland by an arched bridge. It is a major reconstruction of a strong, 13th-century fortress built on the orders of Alexander II to guard over the lands of Kintail. Held by the MacKenzies and later the MacRaes, the original castle, a stone curtain enclosure that received a rectangular great tower, was a stronghold for the Jacobite cause. It was reduced to rubble by a bombardment from Government frigates in 1719 and then stood abandoned for nearly two centuries.

Eilean Donan

Instantly recognizable as the setting of such films as *Highlander* and *The World is Not Enough* this castle is possibly the most photographed in the world. It is better known as Eilean Donan (island of Donan), and most probably named after the Irish saint, Bishop Donan who came to Scotland at the end of the 6th century. There is also a story that the name comes from the Gaelic *Cu-Donn*, or otter (brown dog). An ancient tale recounts that when the King of the Otters died, his fine coat of pure silver and white was buried on the island beneath the foundations of the castle.

The castle rebuilt

Today's castle is the result of a 20th-century reconstruction by Lt Colonel Jon MacRae-Gilstrap, a descendant of the original owners, and his Clerk of Works, Farquhar MacRae.

The castle was rebuilt according to the surviving ground plan of earlier phases – the north wall of the keep was almost entirely renewed, the south wall incorporates much of the earlier structure. It is said that Farquhar MacRae had a vision of the castle and when the old plans were discovered every detail of his dream was faithful to the original. The level of restoration at Eilean Donan was a unique venture – stone was quarried locally, dragged to the shore by horses and taken to the island by boat. The green roof slates came from Caithness and the finished wood and ironwork from Edinburgh. This truly massive undertaking went on throughout World War I and was completed in 1932.

What to see

An introductory exhibition reveals the early life of the castle when it was at the heart of the sea kingdom of the Lords of the Isles. Some of the cannonballs fired during the 1719 bombardment are on display on the ground floor of the keep in the castle's Billeting Room. Above is the Great Hall, which has one of the finest collections of Windsor chairs in the country and timber ceiling beams made of Douglas Fir that were shipped from British Columbia during the restoration – a gift from the MacRaes of Canada. Coats of Arms, which decorate the walls and the fireplace, are all associated with the MacRae family.

Above the Great Hall are the bedrooms, of which none have wardrobes – clean, pressed clothes were brought to family and guests each morning. There is also a door with a carved list of all the Constables of Eilean Donan.

The recreated kitchen

Part of the restoration work included building a kitchen for the castle, as this was, after all, to be the summer home for the family. Visitors can see models of Mrs MacRae-Gilstrap and her staff from the 1930s in the middle of preparing a banquet in the recreated kitchen.

Other attractions

There is a café and a gift shop at the castle and visitors can walk to the nearby village of Dornie. There are wonderful views from the island. A War Memorial on the island commemorates the MacRae clan members who died in World War I.

Location: *Nairn, Highland*

Map ref: *NH 847499*

Tel: *01667 404401*

Web: *www.cawdorcastle.com*

Open: *Daily 10am–5.30pm May–early Oct (last admission 5pm)*

Cawdor

This palatial range of buildings belongs to the Dowager Countess Cawdor, whose family has owned the castle since the 14th century. It was the seat of the Thanes of Calder, an earlier spelling of the place name. They were appointed Sheriffs and Hereditary Constables of the Royal Castle of Nairn, but this has since disappeared. The family also had a residence about 1.5km (1 mile) north-east of the present castle although nothing remains of this small moated fort.

Open to the King

A tall, plain, rectangular four-storeyed tower house was built in the second half of the 14th century. Crenellations and turrets were added in 1454, following a licence to fortify, granted to William Calder by his friend, James II of Scotland. This allowed Calder to erect his castle 'with walls and ditches and [to] equip the summit with turrets and defensive ornaments' but on the understanding that it was always to be open to the King and his successors. The resulting tower was substantial and the lower parts of it have survived, heightened in the 16th century. A deep ditch and a drawbridge were added in the 15th century. The entrance, at first-floor level, had an iron yett. The tower had little strategic importance, it was simply designed as a strong fortified home.

A legendary tree

One of the most unusual things about Cawdor Castle is that it was built around a small tree. The tree, a Holly (although for a long time it was said to be a Hawthorn) died in about 1372, the time when it would have been deprived of daylight. It is possible that the tree was incorporated into the building for superstitious reasons but legend has it that when the Thane of Calder decided to build his stronger castle on a better site, he followed the instructions of a dream and loaded a coffer of gold on to the back of a donkey and let it roam the district for the day. Wherever it lay down to rest was to be the site of the new castle. The donkey lay down under the tree. This legendary dead tree can still be seen in the guardroom of the tower.

A comfortable residence

Later extensions and improvements, beginning in the 17th century, were residential, and this comfortable castle displays a fine collection of furnishings, paintings, tapestries and domestic items. The Tapestry Bedroom, above the Great Hall (now the Drawing Room) was part of the 17th-century civilizing additions. The dressings on the four-poster bed in this room have been recreated from an inventory of 1688. The old kitchen was in use up until the end of the 1930s and is furnished with all manner of utensils – its table was constructed in the room and the well is dug straight into the red sandstone rock.

Gardens and grounds

Cawdor sits in magnificent grounds with three gardens, a wild wood and a 9-hole golf course and putting green, which are all open to the public. Half an hour's walk through the wood is the Cawdor Dower House and Tibetan Garden at Auchindoun. The 5th Earl of Cawdor travelled to Tibet with the explorer Frank Kingdon Ward in the early 1920s in search of the legendary Tsangpo waterfall. They never found it but the Earl brought home a collection of rare Tibetan flora. This was planted in the Dower House gardens to keep it safe from the ministrations of Cawdor's head gardener at the time, who was nicknamed 'Death Ray' and famed for his fatal effect on the estate's plant life. Auchindoune's gardens are open on Tuesdays and Thursdays in May, June and July from 10am–4pm. At Cawdor there are three interesting shops, a snack bar and a licensed restaurant. Wheelchair access is limited.

Location: *Wick, Highland*

Map ref: *ND 369487*

Tel: *01667 460232*

Web: *www.historic-scotland.gov.uk*

Open: *Open access*

Castle of Old Wick

In a dramatic location, the ruins of Old Wick stand precariously on a high promontory jutting out to sea – the best-preserved Viking castle in Scotland. Old Wick was built early in the 13th century, when Caithness was ruled by the Norse Earls of Orkney. Visitors to the site need to take great care, as on either side of the promontory are two deep gullies.

Corgarff

In a wild and lonely setting, the strategic location of this plain rectangular 16th-century tower house has ensured an eventful history. Today Corgarff looks much as it did when it was modified after the second Jacobite Uprising – enclosed inside its distinctive star-shaped perimeter wall. Corgarff was a useful fortress for guarding crossings on the rivers Dee, Don and Avon against smugglers and hostile highlanders. A garrison was maintained here for many years, right up until the 1830s.

Location: *Aberdeenshire*

Map ref: *NJ 254086*

Tel: *01975 651460*

Web: *www.historic-scotland.gov.uk*

Open: *Daily 9.30am–6.30pm Apr–Sep; Sat & Sun 9.30am–4.30pm Oct–Mar*

For the visitor

After falling into disrepair Corgarff was restored in the 1960s and now houses a reconstruction of an 18th-century barrack room, a Visitor Centre and shop. The tower does not have suitable wheelchair access although the adjoining bakehouse and brewhouse are accessible. Visitors with mobility problems can be set down near the entrance by prior arrangement, as the car park is a five-minute walk up a steep hill.

Craigievar

Craigievar, set high on a hill, is a fairytale castle and one of the finest baronial tower houses in Scotland. Built *c*.1610–26, internally Craigievar is simple and homely with a decorated and vaulted roof in the Great Hall. In fact, most of the rooms in the castle have retained their original 1626 ceilings.

A 17th-century castle

Built by William Forbes or 'Danzig Willie', it remains true to its 17th-century origins. Built as a defensible home rather than for purely military purposes, the castle was fortified with ramparts, and a courtyard wall with towers and an outer gateway. There was only one way into the castle – through an iron-studded door, past a yett and through another pair of stout doors.

Location: *Alford, Aberdeenshire*

Map ref: *NJ 566095*

Tel: *013398 83635*

Web: *www.nts.org.uk*

Open: *Please check NTS website*

Inside, the castle has been maintained as it was when the Forbes family left. Belongings collected by the family over the centuries include fine 17th- and 18th-century furniture and Forbes family portraits, as well as a renowned collection of early 20th-century ceramics.

Restoration programme

Craigievar is undergoing restoration so the castle is closed – it is planned to reopen in 2008. After this date, before planning a visit, please either telephone or check the website to ensure the castle has reopened.

Location: *Aberdeenshire*

Map ref: *NO 735968*

Tel: *01330 844525*

Web: *www.nts.org.uk*

Open: *Daily 10am–5.30pm Easter–Sep; daily 10am–4.30pm Oct; Thu–Sun 10am–3.45pm for guided tours Nov–Mar*

Crathes

Crathes is an impressive and much restored tower-house castle known predominantly for its interesting painted ceilings, most notably in the Chamber of the Nine Muses.

Begun as an L-plan tower house in 1553, many of the alterations and improvements were by masons from the Bell family. There were further alterations, including a three-storey east wing, another later wing, and some ornamental corbelled turrets. The original tower was equipped with a luggie, an iron yett by the door and a re-entrant tower for a staircase.

Visiting

There are collections of family portraits and furniture displayed inside the house and a fine garden with several nature trails, one of which is especially suitable for visitors with disabilities. Children will enjoy the adventure playground. A restaurant provides refreshments.

Location: *Isle of Wyre, Orkney Islands*

Map ref: *HY 438261*

Tel: *01856 872856*

Web: *www.visitorkney.com*

Open: *Open access*

Cubbie Roo's

One of the earliest stone castles built in Scotland, Cubbie Roo's tower was constructed in the middle of the 12th century. Enclosed in an oval-shaped earthwork with ditching, Cubbie Roo's was probably the castle (*steinkastala*) built *c*.1145 by the Viking Kolbein Hruga, although the castle takes its name from a giant of Orkney folklore. The castle's remains are of great interest to aficionados and close by there is a well-preserved 12th-century church.

Delgatie

Mary, Queen of Scots stayed at Delgatie after the Battle of Corrichie in 1562 and visitors to the castle can view her room. Although it was rebuilt in *c*.1570, Delgatie's main tower house dates from as early as *c*.1050. Some of the rooms at the castle still have their 16th-century painted ceilings, which are widely considered to be among the finest examples in Scotland. Another arresting feature is the turnpike stairway, built into the thickness of the wall, and notable for its width.

A pleasurable stopover

Delgatie's lovely setting in the heart of Scotland's Castle Trail, its tremendous character, homely atmosphere and its tearoom (which serves a celebrated carrot cake), make for a pleasurable stopover for visitors of all ages. Accommodation is also offered at the castle and there are self-catering cottages available to rent in a converted stable-block in the grounds.

Each year, on the last weekend of November and first weekend of December, the castle adopts a Victorian Christmas theme – there is a visit from Santa and a craft fair.

Location: *Turriff, Aberdeenshire*

Map ref: *NJ 754505*

Tel: *01888 563479*

Web: *www.delgatiecastle.com*

Open: *Daily 10am–5pm all year (closed Xmas and New Year weeks)*

Location: *Near Peterculter, Aberdeenshire*

Map ref: *NJ 796005*

Tel: *01330 811204*

Web: *www.drum-castle.org.uk*

Open: *Daily 12.30pm–5.30pm Apr–May & Sep; daily 10am–5.30pm Jun–Aug. Last entry 45 mins before closing*

Drum

The castle at Drum is a fine example of a late 13th-century great tower, one of the three oldest in Scotland and the only one to remain intact. It has rounded corners and few window openings, a spiral staircase from the first floor up to the battlemented parapet and wall-walk, and adjoins an early 17th-century mansion built by the 9th Laird of Drum. The castle was further altered during Victorian times.

William Irvine, armour-bearer to Robert Bruce, was given the charter to the Royal Forest of Drum in the 1320s but it is likely that the tower was built before the 1280s. Its site, on a ridge above the River Dee, would have afforded protection for nearby Aberdeen.

Visitor attractions

Irvine descendants passed the castle to The National Trust for Scotland in 1976. Inside there are fine portraits and a collection of Georgian furniture. The grounds contain a garden of historic roses, a pond garden and the Old Wood of Drum, an ancient oak wood that is now a Site of Special Scientific Interest.

The castle has a lively atmosphere largely due to the range of events held here, mainly geared to families. There is also a tearoom serving refreshments.

Duffus

Founded by Freskin de Moravia, a Norman-Scottish baron in the reign of David I, Duffus began as a tall motte enclosed by a ditch with a ditch-encircled bailey.

The castle was held by supporters of Edward I and Scottish patriots burned the wooden castle. The motte was given a stone great tower and a stone curtain round the bailey c.1300. In the 15th century a range of buildings was added along the north side of the bailey.

Today the castle is surrounded by flat farmland but when it was built its position was far more strategic, located on the shore of Loch Spynie and surrounded by marshy ground. The castle is now ruinous but it remains one of the finest examples of a motte-and-bailey castle in Scotland.

Location: *Elgin, Moray*

Map ref: *NJ 189672*

Tel: *01667 460232*

Web: *www.historic-scotland.gov.uk*

Open: *Open access*

Dunnottar

Dunnottar Castle sits on a flat-topped promontory surrounded by the North Sea and joined to the mainland by a small low-level isthmus. The approach is likely to be difficult for visitors with disabilities. The site of fortifications for hundreds of years, an earthwork-and-clay castle from the 12th century was used by William the Lion as an administrative centre. At the end of the 14th century an early L-plan tower house was built on the headland.

Location: *Near Stonehaven, Aberdeenshire*

Map ref: *NO 881838*

Tel: *01569 762173*

Web: *www.dunechtestates.co.uk*

Open: *Mon–Sat 9am–6pm, Sun 2pm–5pm Easter–Oct; Fri–Mon 9am–sunset Nov–Easter*

A grand residence

The castle was granted to the Earl Marischals of Scotland in 1531 by James V and became one of Scotland's most palatial residences in the late 16th and early 17th centuries. Besieged by Montrose in 1645 and again in 1651 by Cromwell's forces, Dunnottar was dismantled in the 18th century but the ruins are impressive and some repairs have been carried out.

During Cromwell's time at Edinburgh Castle, the Honours of Scotland – the Crown, Sceptre and Sword of State – were hidden at Dunnottar Castle. This dramatic site, almost surrounded by the sea, was the location for *Hamlet* (1990) starring Mel Gibson.

Location: *Golspie, Highland*

Map ref: *NC 852008*

Tel: *01408 633177*

Web: *www.great-houses-scotland. co.uk*

Open: *Mon–Sat 10.30am–4.30pm, Sun 12pm–4.30pm Apr–May & Oct; Mon–Sat 10.30am–5.30pm, Sun 12pm–5.30pm Jul–Aug*

Dunrobin

This magnificent castle-palace is largely the creation of the 17th and 19th centuries, built on an early 15th-century great tower, which belonged to the Earls of Sutherland (then Morays). The most northerly of Scotland's great houses, in the 17th century the tower was converted to a courtyard-plan castle-mansion. Sir Charles Barry remodelled it in the 19th century.

Splendid attractions

There is much for visitors to see here including paintings, furniture and heirlooms. Queen Victoria stayed here and her room, the Gold and Green Room, can be viewed. The study has secret stairways.

French-style gardens

The style of Dunrobin recalls a French chateau and its formal gardens were inspired by the grounds of the Palace of Versailles. Laid out soon after the additions to the house by Sir Charles Barry, the garden remains much the same as it would have looked originally – two spectacular parterres laid out around circular pools with fountains. A vegetable garden and orchard, again with French influence, were begun at the end of the 20th century. The museum in the grounds has a range of interesting exhibits. There is a tearoom offering a range of refreshments.

Location: *Isle of Skye*

Map ref: *NG 250480*

Tel: *01470 521206*

Web: *www.dunvegancastle.com*

Open: *Daily 10am–5pm mid-Mar–Oct; daily 11am–4pm Nov–mid-Mar*

Dunvegan

This romantic fortress is still occupied by the Chiefs of the MacLeod clan whose ancestors erected it in the Middle Ages. The present structure is a 19th-century transformation of a castle begun in the 13th century and it is possible to see relics from many of the ten building periods. Dunvegan stands on a rock projecting into the sea. One early feature of the castle is the remnant of a sea gate, which was once the only entrance to the castle.

Additional attractions

Displayed inside are MacLeod heirlooms including the bullhorn, which dates from the 14th century. It is still filled with claret for each male heir to the MacLeod Chiefdom, who then has to drain it. The castle gardens were laid out in the 18th century. Today the gardens remain open throughout the year, attracting keen gardeners from around the world. A popular excursion is a boat trip to see the seals in Loch Dunvegan. The restaurant has ramps for wheelchair access.

Fyvie

One of Scotland's great royal fortress-palaces, visited by both Edward I and Robert Bruce, Fyvie has a long and complex building history. The whole south front has a formidable appearance, but is not actually properly fortified and the first mention of stonework at

Location: *Turriff, Aberdeenshire*

Map ref: *NJ 764323*

Tel: *01651 891266*

Web: *www.nts.org.uk*

Open: *Sat–Wed 12pm–5pm Easter–Jun & Sep; daily 11am–5pm Jul–Aug*

the castle is about 1390. The south-east tower (Preston) was built between 1390 and 1430; the south-west tower (Meldrum) some time between 1433 and 1590. The gatehouse dates from the late 16th century. Additions were made right up to the 1890s. This is a perfect example of a castle that continued to be lived in long after there was any need for it to have a defensive function, and is well worth visiting.

For the visitor

Inside, the most famous and notable feature is the wheel staircase, with wide sweeping steps and a solid newel. It is the finest example in Scotland. The opulent interior has excellent collections of portraits, arms and armour. Fyvie's grounds were landscaped in the 19th century – the traditional walled garden has been preserved and is now stocked with fruit and vegetables. A tearoom provides refreshments.

Location: *Near Strathdon, Aberdeenshire*

Map ref: *NJ 397148*

Tel: *01667 460232*

Web: *www.historic-scotland.gov.uk*

Open: *Open access at all reasonable times*

Glenbuchat

Glenbuchat was built in the last decade of the 16th century and is an excellent example of a Z-plan castle with square towers. It was built, overlooking the river Don, for John Gordon and his wife on the occasion of their wedding. This is marked on a stone above the entrance together with a motto. The castle remained in the hands of the powerful Gordon family until the first half of the 18th century. The last Laird of Glenbuchat, also John Gordon, was a hero of both Jacobite Uprisings. Known as Old Glenbuchat, Gordon's devotion to the Pretender's cause was such that George II was haunted by him in his dreams and would wake up screaming 'De gread Glenbogged is goming.'

The entrance to the castle building is in the east wall of the south-west tower, and it had an outer door and an inner yett. The door could not be opened until the yett behind it had been opened. A staircase led up from opposite this entrance to the first floor, where there was access to the spiral staircase in the cylindrical projection – the castle's staircases are supported by squinch-arches and not corbelling. The tower walls were equipped with gun-loops all round. Glenbuchat remained in the hands of the Gordon family until the 18th century; the roof was taken off in the middle of the 19th century.

Making a visit

The castle, which stands in attractive surroundings, is reached via a narrow track leading from the main road. Some restoration work has been undertaken and much of the castle has interesting carved stonework. Visitors can explore the first floor and the vaulted ground floor.

Huntly

Described as one of the noblest baronial ruins in Scotland, this remarkable structure, a mixture of building periods, was the fortified residence of one of the wealthiest and most powerful families in Scotland, the Earls (and later Marquises) of Huntly.

Location: *Aberdeenshire*

Map ref: *NJ 532407*

Tel: *01466 793191*

Web: *www.historic-scotland.gov.uk*

Open: *Daily 9.30am–6.30pm Apr–Sep; Sat–Wed 9.30am–4.30pm Oct–Mar*

The Earls of Huntly

There are the remains of three castles on the site at Huntly, the first was a motte castle built in the 12th century: the mound and some ditching are still there. Then a substantial L-plan tower was built in the bailey at about the end of the 14th century, but only the foundations of this remain. The Gordon family owned Huntly Castle, and by the middle of the 15th century they were created the Earls of Huntly. The 1st Earl, to reflect the family's new importance, built another, more palatial castle – the 'new werk' – south of the L-plan, which was then much modified, altered and repaired during subsequent centuries, but the whole block is fascinating.

The basement is all that remains from the 15th century; the top floor has oriel windows that were put in very early in the 17th century. The façade above and below the oriel window line has an inscription bearing the name of the 5th Earl of Huntly, who by then had become the 1st Marquis of Huntly, and his wife. This Earl joined a revolt against James VI, had his home blown up and then, once reconciled with the King, rebuilt it in an even grander style. By the time Huntly was held by Government troops against the Jacobites in 1746, it had been abandoned and was falling into decay.

The ruins of this castle, which until *c.*1506 was known as the Peel of Strathbogie, remain an impressive testament to its former grandeur.

Inverness

Only part of the curtain wall, a restored well and some earthworks remain of the first stone castle built here in the 12th century, which guarded routes to the Highlands. The castle was captured by the Lords of the Isles in 1491 but was retaken by James IV. It was severely damaged in Mary, Queen of Scots' reign, damaged again during the Civil War, and all but destroyed by the Young Pretender, 'Bonnie Prince Charlie', in 1746.

A 19th-century neo-Norman castle, on the site, is now a courthouse. The Drum Tower displays an exhibition on the castle's history.

Location: *Highland*

Map ref: *NH 666451*

Tel: *01463 243363*

Web: *www.historic-scotland.gov.uk*

Open: *Daily 10.30am–5.30pm May–Sep*

Kildrummy

An early 13th-century, red sandstone castle, Kildrummy was once one of the most imposing castles in Scotland. Built by the Earl of Mar, its strategic location commanded important routes across north-eastern Scotland. It was a substantial D-shaped enclosure with a range of buildings erected along the inner face of the north-west curtain surrounded by banks and ditches.

Edward I stayed here at least twice, on his way south from Elgin – Kildrummy's gatehouse is similar to the gatehouse at Harlech, of one of Edward's 'Ring of Iron' castles in Wales.

Early in the 16th century the estate was handed to the Elphinstone family who added a tower house, known as the Elphinstone Tower. The castle served as a base for the Earl of Mar when he raised the standard to launch the 1715 Jacobite Uprising. At the end of the 19th century, restoration work began on parts of the ruin. There is a model of how it looked in its heyday in the Visitor Centre.

Location: *Near Alford, Aberdeenshire*

Map ref: *NJ 455164*

Tel: *01975 571331*

Web: *www.historic-scotland.gov.uk*

Open: *Daily 9.30am–6.30pm Apr–Sep*

Kinnaird Head

Built by Sir Alexander Fraser of Philort, this is an interesting 16th-century rectangular tower house, which was converted in the 1780s into a lighthouse – the first to be built by the Commissioners of the Northern Lighthouses and also the first on top of a fortified castle. Another tower and further buildings were added early in the 19th century. Although it is still in working order, and remains much as it did when the last lighthouse crew left, Kinnaird Head has been made redundant by an unmanned light nearby.

Today the castle houses a lighthouse museum, which tells the story of the Stevenson family, lighthouse engineers to the world, and the story of the lighthouse service in Scotland. There is also a shop and tearoom, which are accessible to visitors using wheelchairs.

Location: *Fraserburgh, Aberdeenshire*

Map ref: *NJ 999675*

Tel: *01346 511022*

Web: *www.historic-scotland.gov.uk*

Open: *Please telephone for admission prices and opening times*

Kisimul

Kisimul (or Kiessimul) is an enclosure castle dating from the late 12th or early 13th century and stands on a small island. It is the westernmost castle in Scotland, a stronghold of the MacNeils and is the only significant medieval castle surviving in the Western Isles. To withstand sieges, the castle was equipped with two artesian wells and a fish trap. A galley, launched at the first sign of trouble, was berthed alongside.

Painstakingly and expertly restored by architect and 45th Clan Chief, Robert MacNeil, until recently it was a family home and open to the public only for very limited periods – some rooms in the castle are still used by the family on occasions. The restoration work means that Kisimul boasts a surprisingly complete range of buildings within its fortress walls, giving a real flavour of the past.

Location: *Castlebay, Western Isles*

Map ref: *NL 665979*

Tel: *01871 810313*

Web: *www.historic-scotland.gov.uk*

Open: *Daily 9.30am–6.30pm Apr–Sep*

Visiting

Weather permitting, a short boat trip from the pier in Castlebay precedes a visit to Kisimul (the castle's admission price also includes the boat trip) and it is recommended that visitors with mobility problems bring a helper. There are stunning views across Castlebay from the walkway around the curtain walls.

Mey

The Castle of Mey, built in the 1560s was bought by Her Majesty Queen Elizabeth the Queen Mother in 1952, while in mourning after the death of her husband, George VI. Falling for its isolated charm and hearing it was to be abandoned, she decided to save it.

<table>
<tr><td>Location: Thurso, Highland</td></tr>
<tr><td>Map ref: ND 290739</td></tr>
<tr><td>Tel: 01847 851473</td></tr>
<tr><td>Web: www.castleofmey.org.uk</td></tr>
<tr><td>Open: Sat–Thu 10.30am–4pm mid-May–Sep. The castle and grounds are closed for the first two weeks in August</td></tr>
</table>

A passion for gardening

So began the Queen Mother's love affair with the Castle and Gardens of Mey. About 10km (6 miles) west of John o'Groats, it stands on rising ground near the seashore, overlooking the Pentland Firth and the Orkney Islands, a short journey from the port of Scrabster. Having acquired the most northerly castle on mainland Britain, the Queen Mother restored it and created the beautiful gardens that can be seen today. For almost 50 years Her Majesty spent many happy summers at Mey.

Taking the tour

A tour allows a rare opportunity to enjoy the Queen Mother's summer home much as she left it after her last visit in October 2001. The tour passes through the principal rooms and some bedrooms, and includes the traditional Scottish walled garden (mostly planted with vegetables surrounded by fruit and herbaceous borders) and the East Garden created out of a wilderness by the Queen Mother.

In 1996 the Queen Mother created The Queen Elizabeth Castle of Mey Trust so that the castle could continue in perpetuity for the benefit of the people of Caithness.

Muness

Muness earns its place in this book by dint of it
being the most northerly castle in the British Isles.
It is a substantial ruin of a 16th-century Z-plan tower
house with cylindrical towers (at diagonally opposite
corners), and some good architectural detail remains.
Built by Lawrence Bruce, an unpopular Sheriff of
Shetland, the castle was attacked and burned by the French in the 17th century (local
crofters still regularly find cannonballs buried in the peat) and in 1713 it was rented out to
the Dutch East India Company as storage for salvaged cargo from a nearby wreck. Access
to the interior of the castle is by key – a notice at the site tells visitors where to obtain it.

Location: *Isle of Unst, Shetland Islands*

Map ref: *HP 629012*

Tel: *01856 841815*

Web: *www.historic-scotland.gov.uk*

Open: *Access at reasonable times (keyholder)*

Mingary

Begun in the 13th century, Mingary was the seat of
the MacIans of Ardnamurchan. Most of the castle
dates from the 16th to the 18th centuries. The castle
was used by James IV to help contain the power of the
MacDonald Lords of the Isles.

Location: *Near Kilchoan, Highland*

Map ref: *NM 503631*

Tel: *None*

Web: *www.west-highlands.com*

Open: *Open access*

In the 16th century the MacLeans of Duart tried and failed to capture Mingary but the
castle was overwhelmed during the Covenanters wars in the 17th century – it was held for
the Government during the 1745 Jacobite Uprising.

The castle is now ruinous but makes an imposing silhouette overlooking Loch Sunart
and the Island of Mull. The nearby village of Kilchoan is the most westerly settlement on

mainland Britain. Mingary is a similar construction to the ruined castle of Tioram, also on the Ardnamurchan Peninsula, and standing high up on a rocky island in Loch Moidart.

A wreck

In the waters beneath the castle lies a recently discovered wreck. Artefacts recovered from the wreck suggest it may be over three centuries old and this is substantiated by an entry in the diary of a prisoner held at the castle who saw the wrecking of a Parliamentarian Dutch ship in 1644.

Noltland

This unusual castle was founded in the 1560s by the Sheriff of Orkney, Gilbert Balfour, a player in the murders of Cardinal Beaton in 1546 and later Lord Darnley, the second husband of Mary, Queen of Scots. One of the earliest of the Z-plan castles, Noltland is remarkable for the fact that it was designed to have two floors of grand living apartments above two floors of heavily defended fortress – the lower floors of the main block and corner towers are fitted with tiers of gun-ports to give covering fire in all directions.

Location: *Isle of Westray, Orkney Islands*

Map ref: *HY 429488*

Tel: *01856 841815 (Skara Brae)*

Web: *www.historic-scotland.gov.uk*

Open: *Daily 9.30am–6.30pm Jun–Sep*

A well-preserved ruin

There is an impressive spiral staircase in the south-western tower, which was probably a later addition. Visitors can explore the well-preserved albeit ruinous castle for free and there are interpretive boards to explain more of its history.

<table>
<tr><td>

Location: *Near Lerwick, Shetland Islands*

Map ref: *HU 405393*

Tel: *01856 841815*

Web: *www.historic-scotland.gov.uk*

Open: *Mon–Sat 9.30am–5pm during Shetland Woollen Company shop hours; Sun key available from the Royal Hotel*

</td><td>

Scalloway

Scalloway is a four-storeyed, rectangular-plan tower house dating from 1600. Patrick Stewart, Earl of Orkney, a man of violent and cruel disposition, is said to have mixed the blood of his victims with the mortar for his castle at Scalloway. After his death the castle was used as an administrative centre for Shetland and, in the 17th century, as a barracks for Cromwell's troops. Today it is a substantial and partially restored

</td></tr>
</table>

ruin with some fine corbelling, a trademark of the castle's designer Andrew Crawford, who was also responsible for Muness Castle (page 44). Visitors can still get a flavour of the castle's former grandeur although its site, among the modern developments of Scalloway, seems rather incongruous.

<table>
<tr><td>

Tolquhon

A Preston and then a Forbes family castle, the substantial ruins of Tolquhon derive from two main periods, the late 15th century and between 1584 and 1589. The first period saw the construction of the 'auld tour' (old tower), but only the vaulted basement and parts of the first floor of this remain.

</td><td>

Location: *Tarves, Aberdeenshire*

Map ref: *NJ 872286*

Tel: *01651 851286*

Web: *www.historic-scotland.gov.uk*

Open: *Daily 9.30am–6.30pm Apr–Sep; daily 9.30am–4.30pm Oct–Nov. Last entry 30 mins before closing*

</td></tr>
</table>

In 1584, William Forbes enlarged the castle round the old tower. He constructed a substantial irregular quadrangular enclosure with ranges of buildings along the inside of three of its walls. Then he added two further towers, both equipped with gun-ports. The parapet of the 'auld tour' was machicolated. The castle was abandoned at the end of the 19th century. The remains of the buildings are substantial and merit a visit.

Urquhart

Urquhart was a substantial enclosure castle built on the site of a motte castle. It was one of Scotland's largest castles.

Structure of the castle

On a sandstone promontory on the shores of Loch Ness, the enclosure was defended from the landward side by a wide, deep ditch that was crossed by a bridge with high walls on either side and was broken in the middle by a drawbridge. The bridge led out from a massive twin cylindrical-towered gatehouse in the high stone curtain. This curtain survives in part.

At the north-east end of the enclosure is the ruined shell of the great tower whose basement dates from the 14th century. The next storeys are 16th century (probably rebuilding of older work) and the top is 17th century. Gun-ports were inserted in the 16th century. South of the great tower is a range of ruined buildings that once contained the great chamber, hall and kitchen, and at the end of this range is an inlet for the loch water, a landing place and a sea gate.

The castle had a turbulent past. By 1297 Edward I had Urquhart under his control. It was retaken by the Scots in 1303, changed hands twice more, and in 1313 became the property of Randolph, Earl of Moray, one of Robert Bruce's greatest friends and counsellors.

Visiting

This popular castle has an excellent Visitor Centre with audio-visual displays and a model of how the castle would have looked when it was intact. There is much to explore at this evocative site.

<table>
<tr><td>Location: Drumnadrochit, Highland</td></tr>
<tr><td>Map ref: NH 531286</td></tr>
<tr><td>Tel: 01456 450551</td></tr>
<tr><td>Web: www.historic-scotland.gov.uk</td></tr>
<tr><td>Open: Daily 9.30am–6.30pm Apr–Sep; daily 9.30am–4.30pm Oct–Mar</td></tr>
</table>

N
E
S
W
HIGHLAND
ABERDEENSHIRE
Edzell
Brechin
Montrose
Forfar
ANGUS
Blair
PERTH
and
KINROSS
Glamis
Claypotts
Dundee
Broughty
Castle Stalker
Duart
Dunstaffnage
ISLE OF MULL
Kilchurn
Scone
Huntingtower
Megginch
Creiff
Perth
Elcho
Cupar
St Andrews
ARGYLL and BUTE
Drummond
Balvaird
Burleigh
Scotstarvit Tower
Castle Campbell
Falkland Palace
FIFE
Kellie
Inveraray
Lochleven
CLACKMANNANSHIRE
Carnasserie
Doune
Kinross
Ravenscraig
STIRLING
Stirling
Kirkcaldy
EAST DUNBARTONSHIRE
WEST DUNBARTONSHIRE
Aberdour
Castle Sween
Dumbarton
FALKIRK
Edinburgh
EAST LOTHIAN
INVER-CLYDE
REN-FREW-SHIRE
NORTH LANARK-SHIRE
WEST LOTHIAN
MID-LOTHIAN
Glasgow
Rothesay
EAST RENFREW-SHIRE
Skipness
NORTH AYRSHIRE
SOUTH LANARKSHIRE
SCOTTISH BORDERS
EAST AYRSHIRE
SOUTH AYRSHIRE
0   10   20   30 Miles

Central Scotland (North)

The region above the Clyde and the Forth was the seat of the foundation of a united Scotland. To the west, Argyll and Bute's boundaries correspond with the ancient territory of Dalriada, founded by Gaels who came over from Ireland; east of here, in Perth and Kinross, is the Moot Hill at Scone, coronation site of generations of Scottish Kings. Stirling's mighty fortress, standing atop a craggy rock, has guarded the major route to the Highlands since at least the 11th century.

Aberdour

Aberdour is an assemblage of ruins from several periods. It began as a hall house built by Andrew Mortimer and passed through the Earl of Moray and the Douglas family until the 16th century when it belonged to the Regent Morton. After centuries of improvements the castle was damaged by fire towards the end of the 17th century and from then much of it was allowed to deteriorate.

Location: *Fife*

Map ref: *NT 192854*

Tel: *01383 860519*

Web: *www.historic-scotland.gov.uk*

Open: *Daily 9.30am–6.30pm late Mar–Sep; Sat–Wed 9.30am–4.30pm Oct–late Mar. Last entry 30 mins before closing*

Visiting

For today's visitors, there are substantial remains with a painted ceiling and a walled garden. Visitors will enjoy seeing the remains of the original tower house, one of the oldest still-standing masonry castles in Scotland. It is situated at the west end of the keep. A café is open in summer and on winter weekends.

Location: *Perth & Kinross*

Map ref: *NO 169115*

Tel: *01786 431324*

Web: *www.historic-scotland.gov.uk*

Open: *Open access to exterior. Check on the website or by phone for dates of internal viewing*

Balvaird

Balvaird is a very large L-plan tower house perched among the beautiful and remote Ochil Hills. Although it is ruinous, the tower still stands to its full height and makes an impressive sight. The castle was built in 1500 by Sir Andrew Murray and altered and developed over the 16th century. Part of the barmkin (added later than the tower's construction period) remains along with the ruins of other buildings – as well as remnants of the interesting plumbing arrangement.

Visiting

The tower itself is only accessible intermittently, open days are advertised on Historic Scotland's website. When internal viewing is permitted, there are wonderful views over the surrounding countryside from the walkway around the main block. If the tower is shut it is still possible to walk through the remains of the courtyard and appreciate Balvaird's striking silhouette and fine architectural detail, and enjoy the tranquillity of the location.

Broughty

Location: *Broughty Ferry, Dundee*

Map ref: *NO 465304*

Tel: *01382 436916*

Web: *www.dundeecity.gov.uk/ broughtycastle or www.historic- scotland.gov.uk*

Open: *Mon–Sat 10am–4pm, Sun 12.30pm–4pm Apr–Sep; Tue–Sat 10am–4pm, Sun 12.30pm–4pm Oct–Mar*

Broughty has been extensively rebuilt and altered as a result of its long history as a scene of sieges and battles. The castle started as a tower house built, at the end of the 15th century, on a rocky promontory at the mouth of the River Tay. By the end of the 18th century, Broughty was ruinous but in 1855 the castle's strategically important position meant that it was purchased by the War Office as part of the Crimean War effort and rebuilt.

A museum

Today Broughty houses a free museum. Displays include a fascinating account of Broughty Ferry and its people through the ages, the local environment, a history of the Dundee Whalers and an exhibition on life in the castle itself. This makes it particularly enjoyable for families, with plenty for children to enjoy in the exhibitions. There are also magnificent views of Broughty Ferry beach and across the Tay. The museum has a shop and refreshment area but access is very restricted for people with limited mobility and inaccessible for wheelchair users.

Location: *Blair Atholl,
Perth & Kinross*

Map ref: *NN 866662*

Tel: *01796 481207*

Web: *www.blair-castle.co.uk*

Open: *Daily 9.30am–4.30pm
Apr–Oct; Tue & Sat 9.30am–12.30pm
Nov–Mar*

Blair

Blair Castle stands strategically at the gateway to the Grampians and the route north to Inverness. The stronghold is now a grand, white-painted castle, and has been home to the Dukes of Atholl since the beginning of the 18th century, and to family members of the Stewarts and Murrays of Atholl long before that.

A brief family history

The Stewarts received the Earldom of Atholl from James II in 1457 and it was from the exploits of the first Earl (he was sent by James to sort out the troublesome MacDonalds of the Isles) that the family adopted its motto 'Furth fortune and fill the fetters'. The title passed

into the Murray family in 1629. During the Civil War, Blair was a Royalist stronghold and a prime target for Cromwell's troops – they captured it in 1652 and held it for eight years, until Charles II was restored to the throne. The title was then 'upgraded' to that of Marquis and became a Dukedom in 1703 under the aegis of Queen Anne. The present Duke lives in South Africa but returns every May to lead the Atholl Highlanders on their annual parade.

Europe's only private army

'Bonnie Prince Charlie' stayed at Blair during the second Jacobite Uprising, and after the flight of the prince, the castle was taken over by the Hanoverian Government. Queen Victoria spent three weeks at Blair in 1844 and in appreciation of the guard of Athollmen, who attended her during her holiday, granted the Duke and his men her colours and, therefore, the right to bear arms. The Atholl Highlanders are Europe's only remaining private army – a room in the castle is dedicated to the regiment's history.

Development of the castle

The present building is mainly a late 18th-century reconstruction grafted on to the remains of a much earlier complex tower-house castle. The first construction on the site was Cumming's Tower, built *c.*1270. Its appearance provoked outrage as the tower was put up without permission, not by Blair's owner but by a neighbour, John Cumming. However, Cumming's Tower still stands as the oldest and tallest part of the castle.

By the time Mary, Queen of Scots stayed at Blair in 1564, a Great Hall had been added (the present dining room) but it was in the 18th century that the greatest transformation took place when the turrets and castellations were removed and Blair became less fortress and more Georgian mansion. Fine interiors were wrought by the Edinburgh stuccoist Thomas Clayton. The 7th Duke of Atholl restored the crenellations and tower in the 1870s.

Visiting

The castle's interiors reflect the different periods of the building's development: the Entrance Hall is in the Victorian baronial style while the grand baroque taste of the 2nd Duke is evident in the elaborate decoration of the Picture Staircase and other magnificent rooms.

Today's visitors will find much of interest – arms and armour, paintings, furniture and memorabilia. There are several exhibitions. The chambers under the Great Hall commemorate the life and times of the Atholl family in the 16th and 17th centuries. Another room has a collection of Jacobite relics and a Victorian nursery has been recreated from items discovered throughout the castle. Visitors with disabilities can follow a full tour through an audio-visual display, and the ground floor of the castle is accessible to wheelchair users.

The estate and walled garden

Blair stands at the centre of around 1,000 hectares (2,500 acres) of estate land, and a network of way-marked trails provides a choice of walks. There is also a pony trekking centre and the estate plays host to annual International Horse Trials. The ranger service runs occasional children's events. Refreshment can be taken at the castle's self-service restaurant.

Burleigh

Near the northern shore of Loch Leven, on the edge
of the village Milnathort, the early 16th-century tower
of Burleigh stands roofless and makes an impressive
ruin. A stretch of enclosure wall joins on to a
remarkable round corner tower with several interesting
features, including gun-ports and shot-holes but most
notably a square, corbelled out cap-house. The castle
was built by the Balfours and much visited by James IV.

Carnasserie

Carnasserie was once the home of John Carswell, first
Protestant Bishop of the Isles, who translated John
Knox's *Book of Prayer* into Gaelic. This handsome
combined tower house and hall was built in the second
part of the 16th century. It was captured during the
rebellion of the Duke of Argyll in 1685 and burned
down, but the substantial remains include some fine
architectural details.

There is a short climb from the car park.

Location: *Dollar, Clackmannanshire*

Map ref: *NS 961963*

Tel: *01259 742408*

Web: *www.historic-scotland.gov.uk*

Open: *Daily 9.30am–6.30pm Apr–Sep; Sat–Wed 9.30am–4.30pm Oct–Mar*

Castle Campbell

This imposing complex of buildings round a well-preserved rectangular tower is sited on a rocky mound in Dollar Glen. The tower was the earliest stone building and dates from the late 15th century, erected on what may have been the site of a much earlier motte castle.

With four storeys, three of which are vaulted, a pit prison and two entrances, the tower's floors were originally reached by straight-flight mural stairways. A square-plan stair tower with a spiral staircase was built in the 16th century. The ceiling was vaulted at a later date, probably the late 16th century and has masks painted in the stonework. The present roof, which is a much later addition, has helped to keep the tower in such good condition.

The second building period was probably in the first half of the 16th century. The main work was a southern range outside the barmkin of the 15th-century tower. In the late 16th century a shorter range was added to the east, joining the original tower to the south range. A curtain at the west and north-west (with a gateway) completed the quadrangle.

These additions were ruined when the Royalists sacked Castle Campbell in the 1650s. The castle was a stronghold of the Campbells.

Visiting

Although the tower still stands, the adjoining rooms and halls are ruinous. The view across the countryside is excellent. The glen has a wonderful range of wildlife and is a Site of Special Scientific Interest.

Castle Stalker

You can see this castle on a small island in Loch Laich from the road driving from Ballachulish down towards Oban. Access has always been by boat. The building was a rectangular tower house, about 14 x 11m (46 x 36ft), and with walls about 3m (10ft) thick. The entrance was at first-floor level, reached by a wooden ladder, later a stone stairway, and the ground level contained a pit prison.

Stalker was probably built in the 15th century on the site of a 14th-century fortalice belonging to the MacDougalls. These MacDougall lands later became the property of the Stewarts until the 17th century when they passed to the Campbells after a wager.

Castle Stalker fell into disrepair and dereliction in the 19th century when the Campbells built a new home on the mainland, but it was preserved and then fully restored towards the end of the 20th century.

Visting

Visitors arrive by boat for tour of the castle accessed via steps from the beach. The website has a very good virtual tour to whet your appetite.

Location: *Appin, Argyll & Bute*

Map ref: *NM 921473*

Tel: *01383 860519*

Web: *www.castlestalker.com*

Open: *The Castle is open by appointment only. Please call the number given during the relevant period: 6–10 Jun (01631 740 306) 13–17 Jun (01631 730 354) 22–26 Aug (01631 730 234) 29–2 Sep (01631 730 234) 5–9 Sep (01631 730 354). Tours are subject to tides and weather conditions*

Location: *Knapdale, near Tarbert, Argyll & Bute*

Map ref: *NR 712788*

Tel: *0131 668 8800*

Web: *www.historic-scotland.gov.uk*

Open: *Open access*

Castle Sween

The well-preserved ruins of one of Scotland's earliest castles are superbly set on the rocky shores of the east side of Loch Sween guarding the mouth of the loch and looking down the Sound of Jura towards Ireland. Four massive walls surround a courtyard, which would have been lined with lean-to buildings: the walls have projecting buttresses – an unusual feature of a castle in this region – and there is a gateway on the south side, set in a section of approximately 3m (10ft) thick masonry.

History

Castle Sween dates from the mid-12th century (perhaps earlier) and was built by the McSwine family (the name possibly coming from the Viking 'Sweyn' or 'Suibhne'). By the 13th century the clan's lands reached as far as Lochawe in the north and Skipness in the south but Robert Bruce displaced the McSwines and gave the castle to his supporter Angus (MacDonald) of Islay. For a time the castle was owned by the Stewart Earls of Menteith who remodelled some of the structure and built additions outside. Towards the end of the 14th century it was held for the Lords of the Isles, and late in the 15th century the castle passed in to the hands of the Campbells, who held it on behalf of the Crown. The squat three-storey corner tower house was a 13th-century addition and the lower floor contains the remains of a kitchen and bakehouse. The round MacMillan's Tower was built in the north-west corner in the 15th century. The castle was attacked and burned during the Civil War in 1644 by Alisdair MacColla and the Clan Donald – it has been a ruin ever since.

Visiting

The area surrounding the castle ruins offers a perfect place to picnic and enjoy the views. There is a campsite nearby.

Claypotts

Claypotts is one of several dozen Z-plan castles built in Scotland in the 16th and 17th centuries. John Strachan, Lord of Claypotts, built it in the 1570s as a rectangular, gabled, four-storey great tower house of local stone with cylindrical towers grafted diagonally on the north-east and south-west corners.

Location: *Broughty Ferry, Dundee*

Map ref: *NO 457319*

Tel: *01786 431324*

Web: *www.historic-scotland.gov.uk*

Open: *Open access to exterior only. For details of interior viewing contact Historic Scotland*

'Bonnie Dundee'

The towers were topped with overhanging square cap-houses and were large enough to contain rooms all the way up. Each of the towers gives cover to two surfaces of the centre building, which in turn covers both towers so, in theory, it was impossible to approach the castle from any angle without being in a direct line of fire. However, the all-round defensiveness of Claypotts was never put to the test. In the 1620s the castle was sold to Sir William Graham of Claverhouse, and it was his great-grandson, John Graham, who was later famous throughout Scotland as 'Bonnie Dundee'. He became 1st Viscount Dundee, and raised an army to help the cause of James II (and VII) who was driven off the English throne late in 1688 by supporters of William of Orange (William III). When James II was deposed, Claypotts was forfeited to William III who gave it to the Marquis of Douglas.

Visiting

Claypotts remains as an outstanding example of 16th-century Scottish architecture but visitors will usually only be able to enjoy the view from the grounds. Contact Historic Scotland for details of open days for viewing the interior, or visit their website.

Location: *Stirling*

Map ref: *NN 725014*

Tel: *01786 841742*

Web: *www.historic-scotland.gov.uk*

Open: *Daily 9.30am–6.30pm Apr–Sep; Sat–Wed 9.30am–4.30pm Oct–Mar*

Doune

The name Doune is derived from 'dun', the ancient word for a fortified town and there are traces of prehistoric earthworks around this splendid stone enclosure castle. It was built towards the end of the 14th century for Robert Stewart, Duke of Albany and Regent of Scotland from *c*.1396 to 1420. When Albany died in 1420 his son, Murdoch, inherited the castle but he was put to death by James I in 1425 and Doune was taken over by the Crown. It was held for more than a century by royalty and then passed to the Earls of Moray who owned it until it was passed into the care of Historic Scotland in the 1980s.

Visiting the castle

The castle was restored in the first half of the 19th century and then again towards the end of the 20th century. The Duke's Hall, on the first floor above the gateway passage, is laid out much as it would have been in its heyday, and to the west is the vast Great Hall. The castle was one of the locations for the 1975 film *Monty Python and the Holy Grail*.

Drummond

The present keep at Drummond, seat of the Earls of Ancaster, was erected in 1490 by special permission of James IV. Built by Sir John Drummond, it was badly damaged by Cromwell's forces in the 1650s but rebuilt. The mansion house, today mostly Victorian, was originally built in 1689.

Drummond Castle is not open to the public but visitors can still enjoy one of the finest formal gardens in Europe. Together with the multi-faced sundial, the property's most admired feature is its Italianate parterre garden from which visitors have wonderful views.

Location: *Near Crieff, Perth & Kinross*

Map ref: *NN 844180*

Tel: *01764 681433*

Web: *www.drummondcastle gardens.co.uk*

Open: Gardens: *Easter weekend & daily 1pm–6pm May–Oct*

Location: *Isle of Mull, Argyll & Bute*

Map ref: *NM 748354*

Tel: *01680 812 309*

Web: *www.duartcastle.com*

Open: *Daily 10.30am–5.30pm May–Sep. For other opening times please check the castle website*

Duart

Duart Castle stands high on a craggy headland guarding the Sound of Mull, enjoying one of the most spectacular positions on the West Coast of Scotland. It still belongs, as it has since the 14th century, to the Clan Maclean. The first recorded mention of the Macleans of Duart is in a papal dispensation of 1367, which gave their Chief, Lachlan Lubanach Maclean, permission to marry Mary MacDonald, the daughter of the Lord of the Isles and she was given Duart as part of her dowry.

When the castle came to the Macleans it was a simple Norman enclosure (a curtain wall surrounding a courtyard) but Lachlan Lubanach added the existing keep, which forms an integral part of the earlier curtain walls. Successive Macleans continued to alter and improve their stronghold through the centuries.

Ruin and restoration

The Maclean clan's eventful history resulted in Duart being lost to the Duke of Argyll towards the end of the 17th century and after a brief period of being used as a garrison for Government troops, the castle was abandoned and fell into ruin. Early in the 1900s, the 26th Clan Chief, Sir Fitzroy Maclean bought Duart and began an extensive and sympathetic restoration. Another Lachlan Maclean, the present Clan Chief, has carried out more repairs on the castle and, although the main works were completed a little over a decade ago, restoration is still underway.

For the visitor

Visitors can view the dungeons and the state rooms of Duart and enjoy stunning views from the top of the keep and from the headland itself. There is a designated children's trail around the castle and a variety of events are held throughout the opening season – many of these are suitable for children and families. On occasion 'Sir Fitzroy's valet and his housemaid Jeannie' take visitors back to the early 1900s and give guided tours – please check on the castle's website for dates and more information of this and other events. Just below the castle there is a shop, tearoom and car park. The grounds contain a Millennium Wood planted in January 2000, which boasts trees and shrubs that are indigenous to Argyll, and makes for a very pleasant walk.

Arrive by boat

There is a car park at the castle but, weather permitting, it is possible to sail directly to the jetty at Duart from the esplanade at Oban on *The Duchess*; there is also a castle coach which meets the ferry from Oban at Craignure.

Dumbarton

Recorded as a stronghold for longer than any other site in Britain, the castle is built on Dumbarton Rock jutting out into the Clyde. By the early 13th century there is a reference to a castle on the site but the only surviving structure from this is the Portcullis Arch. The history of Dumbarton is one of changing ownership, and it was besieged several times. During the 17th and 18th centuries most of the medieval buildings (which were ruinous) were replaced, providing a base for Government troops during the Jacobite Uprisings and to defend the Clyde against France.

Visiting

An exhibition of military regalia and unusual tombstones is on display. The battlements offer tremendous views but there are a lot of steps.

Location: *West Dunbartonshire*

Map ref: *NS 398744*

Tel: *01389 732167*

Web: *www.historic-scotland.gov.uk*

Open: *Daily 9.30am–6.30pm Apr–Sep; Sat–Wed 9.30am–4.30pm Oct–Mar*

Location: *Oban, Argyll & Bute*

Map ref: *NM 882344*

Tel: *01631 562465*

Web: *www.historic-scotland.gov.uk*

Open: *Mon–Sun 9.30am–6pm Apr–Sep; Sat–Wed 9.30am–4.30pm Oct–Mar*

Dunstaffnage

Dunstaffnage sits on a rock on the edge of the Firth of Lorne and on one side the rock face actually makes up part of the castle wall. The castle originally dates from the 13th century and was occupied until the end of the 1800s. Alexander II and III used the site during their campaigns against the Vikings in the Western Isles. Its importance as a checkpoint to the approach to Glen Mor was also recognized by Edward I. It was captured by Robert Bruce in 1309 from the MacDougalls, who sided with Edward I, and passed to the Campbell family via the first Earl of Argyll and then to his cousin, who became Captain of Dunstaffnage. The family retains ownership. Flora MacDonald was held here after she helped 'Bonnie Prince Charlie'.

Dunstaffnage is on the site of an earlier building of the ancient Kings of Dalriada, where the Stone of Destiny was kept until it was removed to Scone.

Visiting

The ruins of the castle and its 13th-century chapel can be visited today. The wall walk has views across the area. Visitors can also enjoy the woodlands and areas leading to Dunstaffnage Bay.

Edzell

Edzell began as a substantial rectangular L-plan tower house built by the Lindsay family in the early 16th century. Later a quadrangle of buildings was added and connected to the tower by an entrance hall, and in the first years of the 1600s, Sir David Lindsay added a spacious walled garden to the eastern side of the courtyard. Sir David died before his project was completed, but the garden still exists. A bath-house tower and a summer house, which is still intact, were added to the corners of the highly decorated walls of the garden, which is one of the most notable of any British castle.

Location: *Angus*

Map ref: *NO 585691*

Tel: *01356 648631*

Web: *www.historic-scotland.gov.uk*

Open: *Mon–Sun 9.30am–6.30pm Apr–Sep; Sat–Wed 9.30am–4.30pm Oct–Mar*

A peaceful history

As a fortress, Edzell had a peaceful history and it was the scene of various royal visits, including one by Mary, Queen of Scots when she held a Privy Council meeting in the hall. Although fortified, the castle was never besieged but suffered through the misfortune of the families that owned it. Edzell was finally sold to the York Building Company and when it went into liquidation, the company assets, including Edzell, were stripped. The castle then passed into the hands of the Dalhousie family.

Visiting

Today it is an interesting and attractive ruin with a wonderful, well-maintained walled garden, which includes sculptures and carved panels.

Elcho

Elcho is a much restored, massive five-floor tower house of the 16th century. The windows are protected by iron grilles and the walls have gun-ports, but the castle was also designed to provide handsome family accommodation. There is evidence that the tower house was enclosed inside a barmkin with a ditch.

The nearby quarry, now a garden, was flooded and connected to the River Tay, and this would have provided a private dock for the castle.

Visiting Elcho

Visitors can view the interior – the ground and second floors are intact – and go up to the rooftop walkway to enjoy views to the Tay estuary and back up towards Perth from the upper tower.

Location: *Near Perth, Perth & Kinross*

Map ref: *NO 164210*

Tel: *01738 639998*

Web: *www.historic-scotland.gov.uk*

Open: *Daily 9.30am–6.30pm Apr–Sep*

Location: *Cupar, Fife*

Map ref: *NO 253075*

Tel: *01337 857397*

Web: *www.nts.org.uk*

Open: *Mon–Sat 10am–5pm, Sun 1pm–5pm Mar–Oct*

Falkland Palace

It is said that Mary, Queen of Scots spent some of the happiest days of her life in the peaceful surroundings of Falkland Palace, the country retreat of Stewart monarchs. Built near the site of an earlier 13th-century MacDuff castle (the base of which can be seen in the grounds) this magnificent Renaissance edifice was begun by James II in 1450. Mary's father, James V, continued the construction but when her son, James VI, inherited the English throne in 1603 and the Royal Court moved to London, Falkland Palace became neglected and it was set on fire by Cromwell's troops. At the end of the 19th century work was begun to restore the buildings to something of their former elegance. The care and maintenance of Falkland was handed to The National Trust for Scotland in 1952.

Highlights for the visitor

Highlights of the tour include the wonderfully decorated Chapel Royal, the Flemish tapestries and a fine collection of portraits of the Stewart monarchs. The King's Bedroom and the Queen's Room are open to the public. There are also splendid gardens and Britain's oldest tennis court, which dates from 1539. Falkland is not accessible for wheelchair users but an armchair tour via audio wand and guidebook is available and the garden has gravel paths. The charming village of Falkland is an attraction in its own right.

Location: *Angus*

Map ref: *NO 386480*

Tel: *01307 840393*

Web: *www.glamis-castle.co.uk*

Open: *Daily 10am–6pm mid-Mar–Oct; Nov–Dec 11am–5pm*

Glamis

This magnificent mansion of the Earls of Strathmore and Kinghorne, one of the finest in Scotland, conceals a number of earlier structures. In 1372 Robert II granted the site to Sir John Lyon and in about 1400 the second Sir John began to build an L-plan tower house. This had outer defences of walls and flanking towers and was surrounded by a moat.

Remains of the medieval castle are incorporated into the present castle, which evolved during the 17th and 18th centuries. Duncan's Hall, one of the oldest parts of the building, commemorates the murder of King Duncan by Macbeth. In fact the killing took place near Elgin but this is the traditional scene of the crime. Here there is a portrait of Mary, Queen of Scots and her

grandfather James IV – Mary stayed at Glamis in August 1562 and James VI was a frequent visitor before the Union of the Crowns and the Royal Court moved south. The crypt (the lower hall of the 15th-century tower) was where the Lord's retainers would have dined – there is supposedly a sealed secret chamber in the thickness of the walls here, where the Lord of Glamis and Earl of Crawford were said to have played cards with the Devil.

The Queen Mother

Glamis was the childhood home of the late Queen Mother, Lady Elizabeth Bowes Lyon. She married the future George VI in 1923 and was mother to Elizabeth II, and to the late Princess Margaret Rose, who was born here in 1930 (the first royal baby in direct line to the English throne to have been born in Scotland for 300 years). Visitors can see the suite of rooms that Lady Elizabeth's mother, the Countess of Strathmore, arranged for the use of the royal couple on visits 'home'. Princess Margaret's son, Viscount Linley, designed the marquetry screen of Glamis Castle seen in the Drawing Room.

Glamis features in Shakespeare's *Macbeth*, and Shakespeare himself may have visited the castle. It is reputedly haunted by a number of ghosts, and the young Lady Elizabeth and her brother David liked to dress up in sheets to frighten visitors.

Glamis' museums

The Blue Room houses a small museum displaying an eclectic mix of treasures that have been collected at Glamis over the centuries. The Coach House museum includes displays on the construction of the castle and more Strathmore history. The castle restaurant is situated in the old kitchen with its carefully preserved 19th-century ovens, stoves and copper pans, and there are four shops (and a small cricket exhibition) in the recently refurbished Cricket Pavilion.

The Grounds

Visitors approach the castle along a spectacular avenue. The beautiful gardens were landscaped in the early 19th century and, in addition to formal gardens, feature a nature trail and a pinetum, where you might spot a rare red squirrel.

The castle is still a family home, and visitors can join a tour of selected rooms. For anyone who is a fan of the 'Queen Mum' or of the Royal Family in general, a visit to Glamis is essential. Nearby is the charming village of Angus where there is a carved Pictish stone and the Angus Folk Museum, illustrating the life of the villagers in days gone by.

Location: *Perth, Perth & Kinross*

Map ref: *NO 082251*

Tel: *01738 627231*

Web: *www.historic-scotland.gov.uk*

Open: *Mon–Sun 9.30am–6.30pm Apr–Sep; Sat–Wed 9.30am–4.30pm Oct–Mar*

Huntingtower

This tower house is made up from two separate rectangular tower blocks dating from the 15th century, joined by adding walling up to three storeys in the 17th century to form one building. Huntingtower, which was originally known as the House of Ruthven, is perhaps most famous as the scene of the Ruthven Raid of 1582 when William Ruthven, the Earl of Gowrie, and the Earl of Mar, kidnapped the boy-king James VI to get him away from the political and religious influence the Duke of Lennox and the Earl of Arran. William Ruthven was later executed for this treason.

The House of Ruthven was abolished after two later Ruthvens were disgraced, hence the change of name to Huntingtower. The castle then passed to the Earls of Tuillibardine and the Earls of Atholl, who lived here until early in the 19th century.

The castle has exceptional 16th-century painted ceilings, uncovered during restoration work early in the 20th century.

Inveraray

Seat of the Dukes of Argyll, Inveraray Castle is one of Scotland's most famous ancestral homes. The castle, with its French-influenced conical spires, stands majestically on the banks of Loch Fyne. Sir John Vanbrugh, the architect of England's Blenheim Palace and Castle Howard, first outlined the plans for this castle and construction started in 1746. By the time it was finished in 1789 it incorporated Baroque, Gothic and Palladian features and exquisite interiors.

Visitors can wander through the extravagant stately rooms and admire the breathtaking adornment of the Armoury Hall, which has the highest ceiling in Scotland. In contrast, the basement kitchen provides a fascinating insight into life 'below stairs'.

Location: *Argyll & Bute*

Map ref: *NN 094090*

Tel: *01499 302203*

Web: *www.inveraray-castle.com*

Open: *Mon–Sat 10am–5.45pm; Sun 12pm–5.45pm (last admission 5pm) Apr–Oct*

Walks around the estate

The formal gardens around the castle are available to view only by horticultural societies but visitors can enjoy the majestic views from a number of walking routes around the Estate. Follies and fanciful buildings that have been added by successive generations of the family can be appreciated along the way. There is a well-stocked shop and tearoom inside the castle.

Location: *Pittenweem, Fife*

Map ref: *NO 520052*

Tel: *01333 720271*

Web: *www.nts.org.uk*

Open: **Castle:** *daily 1pm–5pm Apr–Oct;* **Garden:** *daily all year 9.30am–5.30pm;* **Grounds:** *daily all year*

Kellie

Owned and developed by the Oliphants between 1360 and 1613, Kellie is a huge T-plan castle and a good example of the domestic architecture of lowland Scotland. Three towers are joined to a main block – the north-west tower is the oldest, the east tower was added later and then a substantial main block, ending in another tower at the south-west, joined the two. James VI stayed a night at Kellie (which was then owned by Sir Thomas Erskine) when he made his only visit to Scotland after inheriting the throne of England. The Lorimer family came to the castle towards the end of the 19th century and it was the architect and designer Sir Robert Lorimer who carried out much of the restoration work – he and his descendants lived at the castle until 1970.

Attractions for visitors

Kellie has some magnificent plaster ceilings and painted panelling, and houses a permanent exhibition of the work of Sir Robert's son, the noted sculptor Hew Lorimer (1907–93). Outside visitors can stroll around the Arts & Crafts gardens or enjoy a picnic elsewhere in the grounds. Children like to head for the adventure playground. There is a shop and tearoom – wheelchair users can access these and the ground floor of the castle. Events are held throughout the year; visit the website for details.

Location: *Loch Awe, Argyll & Bute*

Map ref: *NN 133276*

Tel: *01866 833333 (Loch Awe boats)*

Web: *www.historic-scotland.gov.uk*

Open: *Daily 9.30am–6.30pm Apr–Sep*

Kilchurn

Sited on a peninsula in Loch Awe, Kilchurn Castle stands as a splendid ruin among reeds and marshes. It began as a five-floor, square tower at the east, built in the middle of the 15th century by Colin Campbell of Glenorchy, 1st Earl of Breadalbane. Additions were made during the 16th century, and by the end of the 1600s, there were numerous buildings grouped round a courtyard. Kilchurn was abandoned in the middle of the 18th century and is now a gaunt shadow of its obvious former splendour. Access is by ferry or on foot; the castle is open only in the summer.

Lochleven

This island castle is a romantic and well-preserved ruin of a late 14th- or early 15th-century tower with a courtyard surrounded by a stout barmkin. Mary, Queen of Scots was imprisoned here in 1567 and was forced to abdicate in favour of her son James VI shortly afterwards. She made a dramatic escape from the castle in May 1568.

Late in the 17th century Lochleven was sold to Sir William Bruce, the designer of Edinburgh's Holyrood House, and the architect of the stately Kinross House, which stands directly opposite the castle.

For the visitor

Interpretive panels explain how the site has changed and the role that the castle has played in Scotland's history. Visitors can also take advantage of the tranquillity of the island where there are wooded walks and plenty of picnic places with wonderful views. The island is accessible only by ferry from Kinross so visitors with limited mobility may find access difficult – the ferry is not equipped to take wheelchairs.

Location: *Castle Island, Loch Leven, Perth & Kinross*

Map ref: *NO 137017*

Tel: *07778 040483 (mobile) in the summer, 07767 651566 (mobile) for other times*

Web: *www.historic-scotland.gov.uk*

Open: *Daily 9.30am–6.30pm Apr–Sep*

Megginch

This late 15th-century L-plan tower house with gun-ports, built by the Hay family, became part of a larger and less-fortified structure in the 18th century. The castle was used as a location for the 1995 film *Rob Roy* starring Liam Neeson.

The gardens are renowned and include a fountain parterre, a Gothic courtyard, a walled garden and a water garden. Refreshments are available.

Location: *Near Perth, Perth & Kinross*

Map ref: *NO 242246*

Tel: *01821 642222*

Web: *www.scottishmuseums. org.uk*

Open: *Daily 2pm–5pm Apr–Oct*

Location: *Kirkcaldy, Fife*

Map ref: *NT 290924*

Tel: *0131 6688800*

Web: *www.historic-scotland.gov.uk*

Open: *Open access*

Ravenscraig

Ravenscraig was the first castle in Britain specifically planned for defence with guns. James II of Scotland, who initiated the work in 1460, intended it to be a coastal fortress to guard against any attack from the Firth of Forth. The castle is positioned on a prominent rocky site jutting into Kirkcaldy Bay. A wide, natural gully divides the site from the mainland, and this was artificially extended.

Two towers

There were two huge D-plan towers with 3–4.5m (10–15ft) thick walls. The western tower, whose outer wall stands sheer on a slope down to the beach, is in reality a great tower. It was fortified and residential with mural chambers on each floor, as well as main centre rooms with garderobes.

Both towers were given keyhole gun-ports, some of them designed for falconets (small cannons) and the whole front of the castle presented a formidable array of gun-ports through which the garrison could have discharged the most murderous fire.

The castle's position on the shore meant that, if it was besieged, a garrison could hold out for a very long time because it could be supplied from the sea.

Ravenscraig was never finished, however, James II's widow, Mary of Gueldres, lived in the castle for a time after her husband's death, and the Sinclairs held it until the middle of the 17th century.

What to see

The castle, now in a park, overlooks the sea and the encroaching town. Where once it stood alone on the coast, the castle is no longer isolated. Ravenscraig has several decorative features, such as cable mouldings, armorial panels, gun-loops and decorative stonework.

Location: *Isle of Bute, Argyll & Bute*

Map ref: *NS 088645*

Tel: *01700 502691*

Web: *www.historic-scotland.gov.uk*

Open: *Daily 9.30am–6.30pm Apr–Sep; daily 9.30am–4.30pm Oct–Mar*

Rothesay

The low-level motte at Rothesay was crowned with an imposing circular stone curtain during the 13th century – its circular shape making the stronghold unique among Scottish castles. Four stout cylindrical towers were placed equidistantly round the circumference and a simple but tall square-plan gateway was inserted. Vikings besieged Rothesay in 1228 and the castle changed hands many times until 1263, when King Haakon of Norway and his forces were defeated by Alexander III at the Battle of Largs. When the Stewarts became kings of Scotland in the 14th century, Rothesay passed into royal hands – both Robert II and his son, Robert III, spent time here. James V often visited the castle when he was trying to establish his rule over the Lords of the Isles. Traditionally the monarch's heir apparent takes the title of Duke of Rothesay and His Royal Highness Prince Charles is the current holder.

The castle was burned late in the 17th century but was partly restored by the Marquises of Bute during the 19th and 20th centuries.

Visitor information

Originally Rothesay Castle would have stood by the sea but since the extension of the shoreline in the 19th century the stronghold has been set in the middle of Rothesay town centre. Its imposing outlines are surrounded by a moat inhabited by ducks and swans. As well as a visitor attraction, the castle is the setting for musical events, historical re-enactments and local weddings. Interpretive panels and a model of the castle as it would have been at the height of its importance give visitors a glimpse into the long history of this royal stronghold. Access to the Great Hall and dungeons is difficult for people with limited mobility.

Getting there

There is only one ferry provider to the Isle of Bute, which runs from Wemyss Bay on the mainland. The castle is a few minutes walk from the ferry terminal. For details of ferry crossings see www.calmac.co.uk/bute

Scone

Scone is central to the story of Scotland as Moot Hill, the ancient coronation site of the Scottish monarchs, is in the palace grounds. From the time of Kenneth McAlpin all the Kings of the Scots were crowned on the hill, seated on the Stone of Destiny. The Stone was captured and removed to Westminster Abbey by Edward I at the end of the 13th century where it was installed in the Coronation Chair used by English monarchs. It was returned to Scotland in 1996 and is now held at Edinburgh Castle, but there is a replica on Scone's Moot Hill.

Location: *Perth, Perth & Kinross*

Map ref: *NO 113265*

Tel: *01738 552300*

Web: *www.scone-palace.net*

Open: *Daily 9.30am–5.30pm Apr–Oct; evening and winter tours by arrangement*

A family home

Parts of the original palace are incorporated into the current structure, which was restored and developed as an outstanding Georgian Gothic residence by the 3rd Earl Mansfield at the beginning of the 19th century. One of the oldest parts of the palace open to visitors is the Long Gallery where Charles II, 'Bonnie Prince Charlie' and Queen Victoria have walked. There is an audio-visual presentation to explain Scone's historical significance more fully.

The treasures of Scone

The Mansfield Earls were great collectors and Scone houses some very fine collections of ivories, porcelain, paintings, furniture and clocks among its numerous other treasures. The orchids displayed in the sumptuous state rooms form part of the largest private orchid collection in the country, which has been built up by the current Lord Mansfield.

Plenty to see and do

Children will enjoy the play area and the unique Murray Star Maze in the gardens, which are home to peacocks. Donkeys, sheep and Highland cattle can be seen in nearby fields. A picnic area, coffee shop and restaurant offer plenty of choices for refreshment. There is also a gift and food shop. Wheelchair users can access all of the palace's state rooms.

Location: *Near Cupar, Fife*

Map ref: *NO 370112*

Tel: *01334 653127*

Web: *www.historic-scotland.gov.uk*

Open: *Keys available during the summer months from the nearby NTS Hill of Tarvit Mansion House from 1pm–5pm*

Scotstarvit Tower

Scotstarvit is a fine, well-preserved tower house of L-plan design probably built in the 15th century and remodelled between 1550 and 1579. At one time it was the home of antiquarian Sir John Scott who wrote a book called *Scott of Scotstarvit's Staggering State of Scots Statesmen* (later described by Carlyle as a 'homily on life's nothingness enforced by examples'). The tower is six-storeyed with few windows. A very small wing contains the spiral staircase that runs all the way up and is topped with a stone cap-house.

Skipness

Skipness was an enclosure castle built in the 13th century with a 16th-century tower house in one corner. The castle was used as a stronghold against the Vikings. Today this major medieval fortress is an impressive ruin to explore and has stonework dating from the earliest building period.

At the end of the 15th century it became a stronghold of the Clan Campbell.

Visitors to Skipness should also take in nearby Kilbrannan Chapel, dating from the early 14th century and dedicated to St Brendan. The graveyard has a collection of fine tombstones, including some dating back to medieval times.

Location: *Argyll & Bute*

Map ref: *NR 908578*

Tel: *0131 668 8800*

Web: *www.historic-scotland.gov.uk*

Open: *Open access*

St Andrews

This interesting fortress stands on a rock promontory
to the north-east of the city of St Andrews. The
first stonework was erected late in the 12th century.
Towards the end of the 14th century a major building
programme began. This included erecting a curtain
round the whole enclosure with two new towers and rebuilding the earlier fore tower.

St Andrews later became a favourite residence of royalty – James III was probably born
there in 1451. The next phase of building was in the first half of the 16th century.

Location: *Fife*	
Map ref: *NO 513169*	
Tel: *01334 477196*	
Web: *www.historic-scotland.gov.uk*	
Open: *Daily 9.30am–6.30pm Apr–Sep; daily 9.40am–4.30pm Oct–Mar*	

Siege tunnels

The castle was besieged in 1546–7 following the murder of Cardinal Beaton, Archbishop
of St Andrews, by Protestant infiltrators. The Protestants captured the castle and held out
for a year against the Catholic forces although extensive damage was inflicted on the castle.
It finally fell into ruins after the Reformation.

During the siege the attackers sank a mine through the rock under the castle, tunnelling
towards the fore tower. The defenders heard of this, calculated the tunnel's direction and
sank a counter-mine, hoping to join up with the besiegers' tunnel and fight them The former,
2m (6ft) high and 1.5m (5ft) wide, slants down to pass under the ditch. The counter-mine
is much the same size and it reached the head of the besiegers' mine nearly 12m (39ft) out
from the fore tower where it was begun.

The mine and the counter-mine have survived to this day and visitors can walk (or crawl)
through the tunnels. The Visitor Centre has interpretive panels.

Location: *Stirling*

Map ref: *NS 788941*

Tel: *01786 450000*

Web: *www.historic-scotland.gov.uk*

Open: *Daily 9.30am–6pm Apr–Sep;
daily 9.30am–5pm Oct–Mar*

Stirling

The landscape looks very different today but in medieval times marshes, hills and two rivers rendered Stirling Castle's towering rocky site highly defensible. With central Scotland's major route into the Highlands passing by this craggy site, control of Stirling Castle meant control of much of the country. Its strategic position led to its status as one of the most important fortresses in the kingdom and Stirling represented Scotland's resistance to English aggression in the Middle Ages.

By the time Alexander I died at the castle in 1124 Stirling was an important royal stronghold and later in the same century the fortress was one of the five castles surrendered to Henry II under the 1174 Treaty of Falaise, which made Scotland a feudal possession of England. The treaty was overturned by Richard I in 1189.

Won and lost

During the Scottish Wars of Independence, Stirling Castle was often under attack, its buildings destroyed and then rebuilt. In 1296, it was seized by Edward I during his Scottish campaign. A year later,

William Wallace recovered the castle after the Battle of Stirling Bridge but lost it again in 1298 when the Scottish were defeated at Falkirk. In 1299, the Scots took the fortress again and held it until 1304, the year of the great siege by Edward I. By this time Stirling was the only noteworthy stronghold still under Scottish control and Edward planned his siege with care. For three months the garrison resisted everything Edward threw at it but eventually it surrendered. The English then held the castle for the next ten years, but in 1314 it was yielded to the Scots after their victory nearby at Bannockburn, and then dismantled.

A magnificent residence

The structure that endured so much battering began as a earthwork-and-timber castle. Nothing remains of Stirling's 12th- and 13th-century buildings, the complex that graces the huge rock stems from the 15th century and later. The Great Hall, the largest in Scotland – restored to all its medieval glory at the end of the 20th century – was one of the first and certainly the finest of the 15th-century Renaissance buildings erected in the British Isles.

Stirling was at the centre of the court surrounding James IV and then his son, James V (crowned at Stirling in 1513, aged just 17 months, after his father's death at the Battle of Flodden Field). James V was responsible for the most outstanding building in the castle precincts – the magnificently façaded palace building, erected for his wife, Mary of Guise.

Abdication and rebellion

James and Mary's daughter was crowned Mary, Queen of Scots in the Chapel Royal at Stirling in September 1543 and her son, Prince James, was baptized at the castle in December 1566. Eight months later the castle saw the coronation of the 13-month-old infant after the forced abdication of his mother. James VI largely grew up at Stirling. When he succeeded to the English throne in 1603, James returned only once more, in 1617.

The fortress was strengthened between 1708 and 1714 during the Jacobite Uprisings. These new defences were tested in 1746 when 'Bonnie Prince Charlie' besieged the castle. This was Stirling's last experience of warfare although its military connections remained until 1964 as it became the base for the Argyll and Sutherland Highlanders whose regimental museum remains open to visitors in the King's Old Building. The museum tells the story of the regiment from its foundation at the castle to the present day.

Attractions for the visitor

Restoration of the palace is under way, but the castle is still open to visitors. Audio-visual tours help explain the history and development of the castle. There is a lot to see here and it is really a must for visitors to the area, who can tour the rooms, halls, chapel, kitchens, courtyards, exhibitions and see the uniforms, medals, silver, paintings, colours and pipe banners on display at the Argyll and Sutherland Highlanders Regimental Museum.

The Chapel Royal displays two tapestries from 'The Hunt of the Unicorn' series. A new Castle Exhibition, which has opened in the Queen Anne Casemates gives a detailed insight into the Stewart monarchy and its relevance to the castle's history. A café is open for refreshments and in summer you can sit outside on the café's roof terrace and enjoy the views.

ARGYLL and BUTE
STIRLING
FIFE
North Berwick
Tantallon
Direlton
East Linton
WEST DUN- BARTON- SHIRE
EAST DUN- BARTONSHIRE
FALKIRK
Blackness
Lauriston
Edinburgh
Hailes
Haddington
Lennoxlove
Newark
Port Glasgow
INVER- CLYDE
Linlithgow
WEST LOTHIAN
Edinburgh
Craigmillar
EAST LOTHIAN
RENFREW- SHIRE
NORTH LANARKSHIRE
Crichton
MIDLOTHIAN
Glasgow
Crookston
Bothwell
Largs
Kelburn
EAST RENFREW- SHIRE
NORTH AYRSHIRE
Lochranza
Craignethan
Lanark
Isle of Arran
Irvine
SOUTH LANARKSHIRE
SCOTTISH BORDERS
Brodick
Dean
Kilmarnock
Dundonald
EAST AYRSHIRE
Culzean
Maybole
Dalmellington
SOUTH AYRSHIRE
DUMFRIES and GALLOWAY
Loch Doon
N
W
E
S
0   10   20   30 Miles
0   10   20   30   40   50 Kilometres

Central Scotland (South)

The Scottish Kings established their authority in lowland Scotland where its people regarded Highlanders as savage and untamed. This was the country's most fertile and populated area and was pivotal to Anglo-Scottish history. Scotland's major cities of Glasgow and Edinburgh are located here. Edinburgh Castle, built on the site of an ancient stronghold, has been a major royal fortress since before the reign of David I.

Blackness

Location: *Near Linlithgow, West Lothian*

Map ref: *NT 055803*

Tel: *01506 834807*

Web: *www.historic-scotland.gov.uk*

Open: *Daily 9.30am–6.30pm Apr–Sep; daily 9.30am–4.30pm Oct–Mar*

Set on a rocky outcrop jutting into the waters of the Firth of Forth, Blackness was built by the Crichtons, one of Scotland's most powerful families.

Damaged by Cromwell, it was used as a prison for Covenanters in the 1660s, and for the French during the Napoleonic Wars. At the end of the 19th century it was used as Scotland's main ammunition depot. The army left Blackness in 1918, and the castle was later restored to a more medieval appearance.

Visiting Blackness

Visitors can explore inside and there are spectacular views from the wall walks and the roof of the main tower. Events are run both in the castle and grounds by castle rangers. Cobbles and uneven ground might make viewing awkward for visitors using wheelchairs. Boat owners can now make use of the pier to visit the castle during a day's sailing on the estuary.

Bothwell

Bothwell was an important castle and is still a fine ruin to explore. It was built *c.*1270 by the Moray (later Murray) family, who also owned Duffus Castle.

Partial building

The castle, built on the south bank of the Clyde in red sandstone, had a great tower, or donjon, over 20m (66ft) in diameter and at least 24.5m (80ft) high, with walls about 4.5m (15ft) thick. Although damaged, much of the donjon survives but the original castle was never finished. Foundations have been discovered of parts of a planned curtain wall, gatehouse and other towers. Wide ditches also indicate that a large area was due to be fortified.

Location: *South Lanarkshire*

Map ref: *NS 688593*

Tel: *01698 816894*

Web: *www.historic-scotland.gov.uk*

Open: *Daily 9.30am–6.30pm Apr–Sep; Sat–Wed 9.30am–4.30pm Oct–Mar*

Chequered history

The castle changed hands many times. In the 1290s it fell into English hands after the deposition of John Balliol in 1296 and the next year the Scots attacked and captured Bothwell. By employing a huge 'belfry' or siege tower made of prefabricated parts, Edward I successfully recaptured the castle in 1301. After Robert Bruce's great victory at Bannockburn in 1314, the castle reverted to Scotland. It was captured by the English again *c.*1331, this time by Edward III but a few years later it fell into the Scottish hands of Sir Andrew Murray. Later in the 14th century the castle came into the possession of the 'Black Douglas' family who rebuilt the hall and chapel and erected a new wall from east to west. It was finally abandoned in the 17th century.

Brodick

The red sandstone Brodick Castle stands on the site of a Viking fortress. In the 13th or 14th century a stone L-plan tower house was built as a seat for the Dukes of Hamilton. The north wing is all that remains of the original building, and the remainder of the structure, dating mainly from the 19th century, was designed by Gillespie Graham.

Outstanding for visitors

A collection of furniture, paintings and sporting memorabilia is on display in the castle, and the garden has an internationally acclaimed rhododendron collection. It is a fine example of a stately home embracing varied elements. The Country Park, which welcomes visitors all year round, is highly acclaimed.

Location: *Isle of Arran*

Map ref: *NS 007379*

Tel: *01770 302202*

Web: *www.nts.org.uk*

Open: **Castle:** *daily 11am–4.30pm (3.30pm in Oct) Apr–Oct;* **Walled Garden:** *daily 9.30am–5pm*

Location: *Edinburgh*

Map ref: *NT 283705*

Tel: *0131 661 4445*

Web: *www.historic-scotland.gov.uk*

Open: *Daily 9.30am–6.30pm Apr–Sep; Sat–Wed 9.30am–4.30pm Oct–Mar*

Craigmillar

This castle was the site for the murder of Lord Darnley, husband of Mary, Queen of Scots, was planned while the queen was staying there. The castle began in the late 14th century as a large L-plan tower house and was built with close-texture rubble of red-grey sandstone, with long, dressed quoins. The great tower house was strengthened in the 1420s by the addition of a massive fortified enclosure with round flanking towers, and other additions were made in the 16th and 17th centuries.

The murder plot

Craigmillar was attacked and burned by the Earl of Hertford on behalf of Henry VIII in 1544, but it was restored in time for Mary, Queen of Scots to reside there from 1566–7 after the murder of her secretary, David Rizzio. During her stay, a band of conspirators, Argyll, Huntly, Bothwell, Maitland and Gilbert Balfour, met and plotted to ensure that 'sic ane young fool and proud tirrane suld not reign nor bear reull over thame' and that '… he sould be put off, by ane way or uther …' – Darnley was to be dispatched.

For the visitor

The castle is an impressive and substantial ruin that invites exploration. You can still climb to the roof of the tower house and enjoy panoramic views. Access, parking and the grounds have all been improved at Craigmillar recently to make it a very pleasant spot for picnics.

Location: *Near Lanark, South Lanarkshire*

Map ref: *NS 815463*

Tel: *01555 860364*

Web: *www.historic-scotland.gov.uk*

Open: *Daily 9.30am–6.30pm Apr–Sep; daily 9.30am–4.30pm Oct–Mar*

Craignethan

This castle stands on a rocky promontory overlooking the River Nethan. It was once a powerful structure built to incorporate artillery defences and it makes an impressive ruin that is well worth visiting today. It consists of a 16th-century rectangular outer courtyard surrounded on three sides by a curtain wall; on the east side the yard is protected by a ditch. In the west wall is a fine battlemented gateway defended at low level by gun-ports. A century after the courtyard was built a private house was erected in the south-west corner: to the east of this courtyard is the older part of the castle, built mostly between c. 1530 and 1545, which consists of a second courtyard surrounded by thick barmkin with towers on the east. The principal feature of the inner courtyard was the substantial tower house which still stands.

Built by Sir James Hamilton in the first half of the 16th century, Craignethan was the last great defensive castle to be built in Scotland and it has a unique caponier (a stone vaulted artillery chamber) which runs across the defensive ditch in front of the tower house.

At one time there was a massive rampart protecting the tower from artillery bombardments but only the base remains. The superlative defences show how the Hamilton family were among the movers and shakers of Scottish history and made powerful enemies. The family backed Mary, Queen of Scots against the forces of James VI's regents, and the castle was slighted in *c.*1580.

A picturesque setting

Craignethan Castle ruins are substantial and make most interesting viewing. The drive to the castle (through pretty winding minor roads) and its picturesque setting are an added attraction. A tearoom provides refreshments and souvenirs are available at the shop. Visitors with wheelchairs can access both the outer and inner courtyards and the ground floor of the tower.

Crichton

Crichton Castle is a formidable structure dating from several periods in history. Its buildings range round a square courtyard, and from the top of the old tower house it is possible to see Borthwick Castle, another fine tower house.

Location: *Midlothian*

Map ref: *NT 380611*

Tel: *01875 320017*

Web: *www.historic-scotland.gov.uk*

Open: *Daily 9.30am–6.30pm Apr–Sep*

Various building periods

The castle now has little more than its walls but it is possible to trace the various building periods. The first structure was a rectangular tower house, probably built by John de Crichton towards the end of the 14th century and originally surrounded by a barmkin. The basement is vaulted, and has a prison cell and a kitchen. In the 15th century the once massive gatehouse tower at the south-west was built by John de Crichton's son, William, who became Lord Chancellor and who virtually managed Scotland during some of the minority of James II. Further alterations were made in the 15th century.

The castle was besieged and captured in 1559 in the struggle between Protestants and Catholics during the Scottish Reformation. Later in the 16th century, Francis, Earl of Bothwell, a cousin of Mary, Queen of Scots, who had spent time in Spain and Italy, transformed the castle into a Renaissance mansion including a notable diamond-faceted stonework façade on the north range.

Location: *Pollok, Glasgow*

Map ref: *NS 525627*

Tel: *0141 883 9606*

Web: *www.historic-scotland.gov.uk*

Open: *Open access*

Crookston

This was a substantial rectangular tower-house castle whose origins go back to the late 12th century, although the tower dates from the 15th century. Its plan was a rectangular tower with four rectangular corner towers – the northeast tower is still largely intact and there is access to the roof where there are wonderful views of the south of Glasgow. Crookston is the subject of various literary references and for a time belonged to the Darnley Stuarts. It has been suggested that it was under the Yew Tree at Crookston that Henry Stuart (Lord Darnley) proposed to Mary, Queen of Scots.

Location: *Maybole, South Ayrshire*

Map ref: *NS 232103*

Tel: *0870 118 1945*

Web: *www.culzeanexperience.org*

Open: **Castle:** *daily 10.30am–5pm (last admission 4pm) Apr–Oct;* **Country Park:** *daily 9am–dusk all year;* **Shops and Restaurants:** *Thu–Sun 11am–4pm Nov–Mar*

Culzean

Culzean Castle and Country Park is The National Trust for Scotland's most visited property. It was originally built as a medieval cliff-top tower house and was transformed into a grand, elegant stately home in the 18th century for one of Scotland's oldest families, the Kennedy 'Earls of Cassillis'. The 9th Earl, Thomas Kennedy, returned from his Grand Tour in the 1750s

and set about making Culzean Castle the family's principle seat – he began the alterations from defensive stronghold to sophisticated residence. It was the 10th Earl, though, who commissioned the famous Scottish architect Robert Adam to create a building that reflected the family's importance. Adam's romantic vision for Culzean resulted in the outstanding architecture and interiors that visitors enjoy today. However, it proved an expensive undertaking for the Earl.

Castle highlights

Although there were further additions and alterations to the castle in the 19th century, Robert Adam's work is still the overwhelming influence at Culzean and there are fine examples of Adam's work throughout the castle. The exquisite oval staircase, the splendour of the Round Drawing Room (or Saloon) with its panoramic sea views, and the Library, designed within the walls of the 16th-century tower house, are just some of the highlights. Tables, chairs, mirrors, candle sconces, wonderful plaster ceilings and marble fireplaces all reflect the taste of possibly the most important British architect of the late 18th century, who was equally well known as a decorator and furniture designer. Adam also designed the home farm and the viaduct, and redesigned the clock tower and stables.

Another important feature at Culzean is the display of flintlock pistols, the second largest collection of its type in existence (the largest is at Windsor Castle). The 12th Earl bought the pistols from the Office of Ordnance at the beginning of the 19th century and had them transported from the Tower of London.

The estate was handed to The National Trust for Scotland in 1945 along with a stipulation, made by the 5th Marquis, that the top floor of the castle should be gifted to General Eisenhower for his lifetime, as a gesture of gratitude from the Scottish people for his role in commanding Scottish battalions during World War II. The Eisenhower Apartment is now operated as a superbly furnished country house 'hotel'. There is an Eisenhower exhibition on the first floor of the castle.

Plenty to enjoy

The vast Country Park offers plenty to occupy visitors – there are magnificent formal gardens to stroll around, 5km (3 miles) of beaches, an enchanting walled garden, a 12 hectare (30 acre) pond which was once used for breeding swans, an adventure playground and extensive way-marked paths through majestic woodlands. Culzean has a choice of refreshment outlets (and plenty of places for a picnic), a Visitor Centre, four shops (including a second-hand bookshop) and
a plant sales centre.

The castle is accessible for wheelchair users and there are motorized scooters available for people with mobility difficulties (book in advance from the Visitor Centre).

Location: *Near Kilmarnock, East Ayrshire*

Map ref: *NS 437394*

Tel: *01563 522702*

Web: *www.deancastle.com*

Open: **Visitor Centre:** *daily 11am–5pm Apr–Oct; daily 11am–4pm Nov–Mar;* **Country Park:** *Daily all year*

Dean

The seat of the Lords of Kilmarnock is concealed within a valley where the Fenwick and Borland waters enter lowland Ayrshire. The Boyd family received the barony of Kilmarnock from Robert Bruce, after their support during the Wars of Independence and the castle was gifted to the Burgh of Kilmarnock in 1975.

Visiting

The building is now a museum and visitor attraction within Dean Castle Country Park. The castle houses collections of arms, armour and tapestries, and is also home to an internationally important collection of early musical instruments. There is a tearoom in the Visitor Centre.

Dirleton

Dirleton began as an earthwork-and-timber castle built by the Norman de Vaux family who were encouraged to settle in Scotland by David I in the 12th century.

In 1298 the castle was besieged on Edward I's orders. The garrison was compelled to surrender; but later it was retaken and then slighted by Robert Bruce.

During the 17th century Royalists used the castle as a refuge and in 1650, General Lambert besieged the castle on behalf of Cromwell and slighted it.

Location: *East Lothian*

Map ref: *NT 516839*

Tel: *01620 850330*

Web: *www.historic-scotland.gov.uk*

Open: *Daily 9.30am–6.30pm Apr–Sep; daily 9.30am–4.30pm Oct–Mar*

For the visitor

Although a ruin, the castle is still impressive and the gardens are a real attraction. The early 20th-century Arts & Crafts garden has what is claimed to be the world's longest herbaceous border.

You approach the castle ruins through the garden, where you will see the large beehive-shaped dovecot, which would have supplied the castle with meat.

Dundonald

These substantial ruins are largely of a fortified tower house built for Robert II late in the 14th century to mark his accession to the Scottish throne. They are the remains of the third stronghold built on this hill. Originally, in the 12th century, an earthwork-

Location: *South Ayrshire*

Map ref: *NS 363345*

Tel: *01563 851489*

Web: *www.dundonaldcastle.org.uk (www.historic-scotland.gov.uk)*

Open: *Daily 10am–5pm Apr–Oct*

and-timber fortress was erected, which was replaced with a mighty stone castle in the 13th century – the well and the stump of a tower from this castle can still be seen. The castle was one of Robert II's favourite residences and he died here in 1390. Dundonald passed out of royal hands in 1482 and the building was ruinous by the end of the 17th century although there is still a good deal to investigate.

What to see and do

Look out for the stone heraldic shields carved into the outside of the castle's west wall – these are among the oldest in Scotland and there are also full-colour representations of them in the Visitor Centre at the foot of the hill. If you are moderately fit, all parts of the castle will be accessible to you.

The Visitor Centre houses an interpretive exhibition and detailed models of the castles that have stood on the site, plus a café and shop. The castle overlooks a children's play area and purpose-built skateboard park and there is a pleasant walk through ancient woodlands to the ruins of nearby Auchans House. Visitors with impaired mobility may find the steep climb up the hill to the castle difficult, however the Visitor Centre is fully accessible.

Location: *Edinburgh*

Map ref: *NT 252374*

Tel: *0131 225 9846*

Web: *www.historic-scotland.gov.uk*

Open: *Daily 9.30am–6pm Mar–Oct; daily 9.30am–5pm Nov–Feb*

Edinburgh

The history of Edinburgh's craggy fortress, entwined with that of Scotland itself, reaches back for thousands of years.

A major royal fortress

At the end of the 11th century this royal stronghold was known as the Castle of Maidens. During the reign of David I the castle emerged as a major royal fortress; it was here that the first recorded assembly of the forerunner of today's Scottish Parliament took place in 1140 and it was David I who built the tiny

St Margaret's Chapel (named for his mother), which still exists as the oldest surviving building in the castle precincts.

Most of the buildings were rebuilt in stone during the 13th century before Edward I's campaign in Scotland. Nevertheless Edward captured the castle in 1296 and the great Scottish fortress fell, not for the first time or the last, into English hands. It was Robert Bruce's son, David II who then rebuilt the fortress after it was finally back in Scottish hands and remnants of the 14th-century David's Tower still lie beneath the 16th-century Half-Moon Battery.

Symbol of the capital

Much of the medieval castle was destroyed in the 'Lang Siege' of 1571–3 and more still in the 17th century when Cromwell set up his Scottish headquarters here and the castle's role shifted from palace to garrison. Many of the castle's extant buildings date from this time and later, although the main courtyard, Crown Square, was begun during the 15th and 16th centuries. Built over vast stone cellars (used at various times to incarcerate prisoners of war) the square contains the most important castle buildings including the Royal Palace and Great Hall. The creation of Edinburgh as the Scottish capital during the reign of James III meant that, like England's Tower of London, the fortress was to serve as the realm's chief arsenal, home to the Honours of Scotland and repository of the state archives.

Prisoners of War

Edinburgh Castle has been used as a prison since the beginning of the 12th century. There were varying standards of captivity for different classes of prisoner – peasants were probably thrown into a dark pit while miscreant nobility would have been under house arrest in a guest apartment.

At the end of the 15th century, when the stone vaults were built, the castle became one of Edinburgh's state prisons.

When Britain and America were at war in the 18th century, American prisoners were held here (as well as many other nationalities) and one of the castle's newest exhibitions, in the prison vaults, recreates the conditions of these captives.

Visiting the castle

The ancient Honours of Scotland – the Crown, Sceptre and Sword of State – are displayed in the Crown Room. Other highlights are the Stone of Destiny, Mons Meg, a massive medieval siege gun presented to James II, the National War Museum and The One O'Clock Gun, fired daily from Mills Mount Battery.

Many of the castle's major sights are accessible to wheelchair users. Two stylish cafes, serving home-cooked food, provide refreshments and there are several shops. The views of Edinburgh from the castle battlements are magnificent.

Each August, Edinburgh Castle's Esplanade is the scene of a world-renowned Military Tattoo (pictured here). The Tattoo closes with the appearance of a lone piper on the battlements.

Hailes

Hailes Castle is an impressive a ruin on the River Tyne. It is one of the few Scottish castles that has remnants of its 13th-century origins and is thought to contain some of the oldest standing stonework in the country. This is found in the lower part of the tower in the north range of buildings, where there is a pit prison and a dovecote. The de Gourlay family put up these early buildings but they supported the English during the Wars of Independence, so in the 14th century the castle was granted to the wild, dangerous Hepburns, later the Earls of Bothwell.

Lord Bothwell and Mary, Queen of Scots

The Hepburns added buildings, including a substantial square-plan tower at the west and lofty curtain walls, much of which can be seen, though in a dilapidated state. James Hepburn, the 4th Earl of Bothwell was involved in the murder of Lord Darnley. He then married Mary, Queen of Scots, a union that led to Mary's forced abdication, to Bothwell's flight into exile and to the forfeiture of all his lands including Hailes. The castle was dismantled by Cromwell in 1650 although there is still a surprising amount to explore and it is set in beautiful surroundings.

Location: *Near East Linton, East Lothian*

Map ref: *NT 574757*

Tel: *0131 668 8800*

Web: *www.historic-scotland.gov.uk*

Open: *Open access*

Kelburn

Kelburn Castle has been home to the Boyle family for many centuries and is thought to be the oldest castle in Scotland to have been continuously inhabited by the same family. A late 16th-century tower house incorporates the original Norman keep. Late in the 17th century further palatial buildings were added as the Boyle family became more influential.

Although still used as a family home, visitors can view it by guided tour for two months of the year. The grounds have been turned into a Country Park.

Location: *Near Largs, North Ayrshire*

Map ref: *NS 217567*

Tel: *01475 568 685*

Web: *www.kelburncountrycentre. com*

Open: *Daily 10am–6pm Easter–Oct;* **Castle Tours:** *Aug & Sep;* **Grounds/Riding School:** *daily all year*

The Country Park

Kelburn's Country Centre offers a wealth of attractions. In the grounds there are some of Scotland's most famous trees including a pair of yews thought to be over 1,000 years old. A wonderful walled garden and a spectacular glen and burn are other attractions, although children will be particularly enchanted by the Secret Forest – an area of woodland that is full of surprises. There are also several play areas, birds of prey, a riding school, pottery workshop, exhibition centre, café and shop. Events are run throughout the season, many of them especially for children. Visit the website for further details.

Location: *Edinburgh*

Map ref: *NT 204762*

Tel: *0131 336 2060*

Web: *www.cac.org.uk*

Open: **Castle admission by guided tour only:** *Sat–Thu (last tour 4.20pm) Apr–Oct; Sat & Sun pm only Nov–Mar; contact the Steward for tour times;* **Grounds:** *daily 9am–dusk all year*

Lauriston

Lauriston is an early 19th-century mansion grafted round a late 16th-century tower house, built for Sir Archibald Napier, but the Lauriston of today looks less castle than it does large suburban villa.

Edwardian interiors

The mansion was left to the nation in the 1920s by Mr and Mrs William Robert Reid, and displays Edwardian period interiors together with an eclectic mix of furniture and objets d'art collected by its last private owners, transporting visitors back to wealthy middle-class life in the early 20th century.

Only 5km (3 miles) from Edinburgh city centre, Lauriston hosts an annual programme of events from Spring until Christmas, and is in an idyllic setting surrounded by 12 hectares (30 acres) of parkland and formal gardens with spectacular views of the Firth of Forth. A Japanese garden was completed in 2002 and admission to the grounds is free.

Location: *Haddington, East Lothian*

Map ref: *NT 514 720*

Tel: *01620 823720*

Web: *www.lennoxlove.org*

Open: *Closed until Jul 2007 for refurbishment. Wed, Thu & Sun 1.30pm–4.30pm Easter–end Oct*

Lennoxlove

This used to be known as Lethington Castle because it belonged to the Maitlands of Lethington (William Maitland was 'Mr Secretary' Maitland, the Protestant statesman in the time of Mary, Queen of Scots; John Maitland became Lord Chancellor of Scotland in the reign of James VI and was the first Lord Thirlestane). It began as an L-plan tower well before 1400. The castle has been much altered through the centuries, the famous Scottish architect Robert Lorimer carried out some of the work early in the 20th century, but among the original features are dungeons and two iron yetts.

A name change

Late in the 17th century Lethington was sold to the trustees of the Duchess of Lennox and Richmond who had left money to buy a house for her nephew, Lord Blantyre, on condition that it was called 'Lennox's Love to Blantyre'. In time the castle came to be known as Lennoxlove. The Duke of Hamilton bought the castle in the 1940s and the family still lives there. A fabulous collection of memorabilia, which includes Mary, Queen of Scots' death mask, is on display at the castle and can be viewed on a guided tour.

Lithlingow

Sited on a mound overlooking Linlithgow Loch, this is the ruin of a great palace castle. It is roofless but has most of its walling, still showing its impressive size and architecture. The basement, ground and first floors are accessible to visitors, as is Queen Margaret's Bower, high up and with views of the surrounding country-side. The fabric is of several building periods, from the 1400s to the 1600s.

Location: *West Lothian*

Map ref: *NS 996774*

Tel: *01506 842896*

Web: *www.historic-scotland.gov.uk*

Open: *Daily 9.30am–6.30pm Apr–Sep; daily 9.30am–4.30pm Oct–Mar*

A royal residence

Linlithgow may have begun as a royal manor house for Scottish Kings, first of all for David I. The site fell into English hands in *c*.1300, and in 1302–3 an enclosure with turrets made of 'great logs not split too small' was erected on the mound by the order of Edward I and under the supervision of Master James of St George. The castle was besieged in 1303 but was not taken.

After the Battle of Bannockburn, just over a decade later, the castle was returned to the Scots and continued as a royal residence. In 1425, after a damaging fire, James I decided to build a fortified palace on the site and during the next decade more than £4,500 was spent.

The structure that emerged under the aegis of several Kings was a fine mix of the best contemporary residential apartments and up-to-date fortifications. On the first floor of the eastern side is the 15th-century Lyon Chamber. The northern side of Linlithgow was reconstructed in the 1620s and the resulting Renaissance-style range is known as the New Wark. After the Union of the Crowns the Court moved to London. The palace, the birthplace of Mary, Queen of Scots, was damaged by fire in the 18th century and never restored.

Location: *Dalmellington, East Ayrshire*

Map ref: *NX 484950*

Tel: *0131 668 8800*

Web: *www.historic-scotland.gov.uk*

Open: *Open access*

Loch Doon

This unusual eleven-sided enclosure castle was built in the very late 13th century on an island in Loch Doon. It was originally a stronghold of the Earls of Carrick and despite its position in the middle of a deep, wide, loch it was besieged several times. By 1510 it was in Kennedy hands but the castle was destroyed in the 16th century by James V as part of an attempt to reduce the power of his barons. In the 1930s the ruins were moved piece by piece to the west shore of the loch because the water level was to be raised to service a hydroelectric scheme. The superlative setting of this castle in the heart of the Galloway Forest Park makes it almost impossible not to combine a visit with a walk or cycle ride. There is a car park and information board beside the ruins and a tearoom nearby.

Lochranza

The substantial remains of this once royal castle stand on a grassy spit of land jutting into the small sea inlet of Loch Ranza, against a backdrop of splendid mountains. The original building dates from the 13th

Location: *Isle of Arran*

Map ref: *NR 931506*

Tel: *0131 668 8800*

Web: *www.historic-scotland.gov.uk*

Open: *Open access*

century and it is believed that Robert Bruce landed at Lochranza on his return from Ireland to claim the Scottish throne. By late in the 14th century the castle belonged to Robert II, who used it as a hunting lodge and it was a base for James IV in his campaign against the Lords of the Isles. The remains that stand today date from a 16th-century reconstruction. By 1705 the castle had become the property of the Hamilton family but became disused and dilapidated by the end of the 18th century. Another of the attractions of Lochranza village is the whisky distillery with its award-winning café and restaurant.

Location: *Port Glasgow, Inverclyde*

Map ref: *NS 328745*

Tel: *01475 741858*

Web: *www.historic-scotland.gov.uk*

Open: *Daily 9.30am–6.30pm Apr–Sep*

Newark

These days the well-preserved Newark Castle has an unusual location in the shipyards of Port Glasgow, with a frontage on to the River Clyde. When it was first built, in the 15th century, it would have been set in a much greater area and surrounded by a barmkin of which the dovecot was one of its original corner towers. A Renaissance mansion was added, to link the tower and gatehouse, and the barmkin was demolished (except for the dovecot) in the 16th century. The castle was enlarged to accommodate the sizeable family of its notorious resident Patrick Maxell – a friend of James VI, a murderer (he killed two members of a rival family) and a wife-beater.

A hidden treasure

The castle began to be surrounded by shipyards in the 17th century and until the 1980s it was a hidden treasure used by local businesses for storage and workshops. Now though it is a worthy visitor attraction with plenty to explore and wonderful views from the tower. There is a shop. Only the ground floor is accessible to wheelchair users.

Location: *North Berwick, East Lothian*

Map ref: *NT 595850*

Tel: *01620 892727*

Web: *www.historic-scotland.gov.uk*

Open: *Daily 9.30am–6.30pm Apr–Sep; Sat–Wed 9.30am–4.30pm Oct–Mar*

Tantallon

This is a fascinating and powerful castle on a coastal site. It sits on a promontory with three of its sides jutting into the Firth of Forth and below high, sheer rock cliffs falling straight down to the sea. On the fourth side, a ditch about 6m (20ft) wide is cut into the rock. Inside the ditch is a massive 15m (50ft) tall and 3.5m (10ft) thick battlemented curtain wall of dressed red freestone.

In the curtain is a central mid-tower containing the entrance and remains of end towers at the north-west and south-east. The ruins of all three towers rise to nearly 24.5m (83ft). The gatehouse tower had four floors of residential accommodation above the room that contained the portcullis mechanism and consisted at the front of a pair of square-plan wings up to the second floor.

This structure, together with a two-hall block at the north, dates from the 14th century when the castle was in the hands of the 'Black Douglas' family. Tantallon was attacked and bombarded by Cromwell's troops in 1651, and then abandoned.

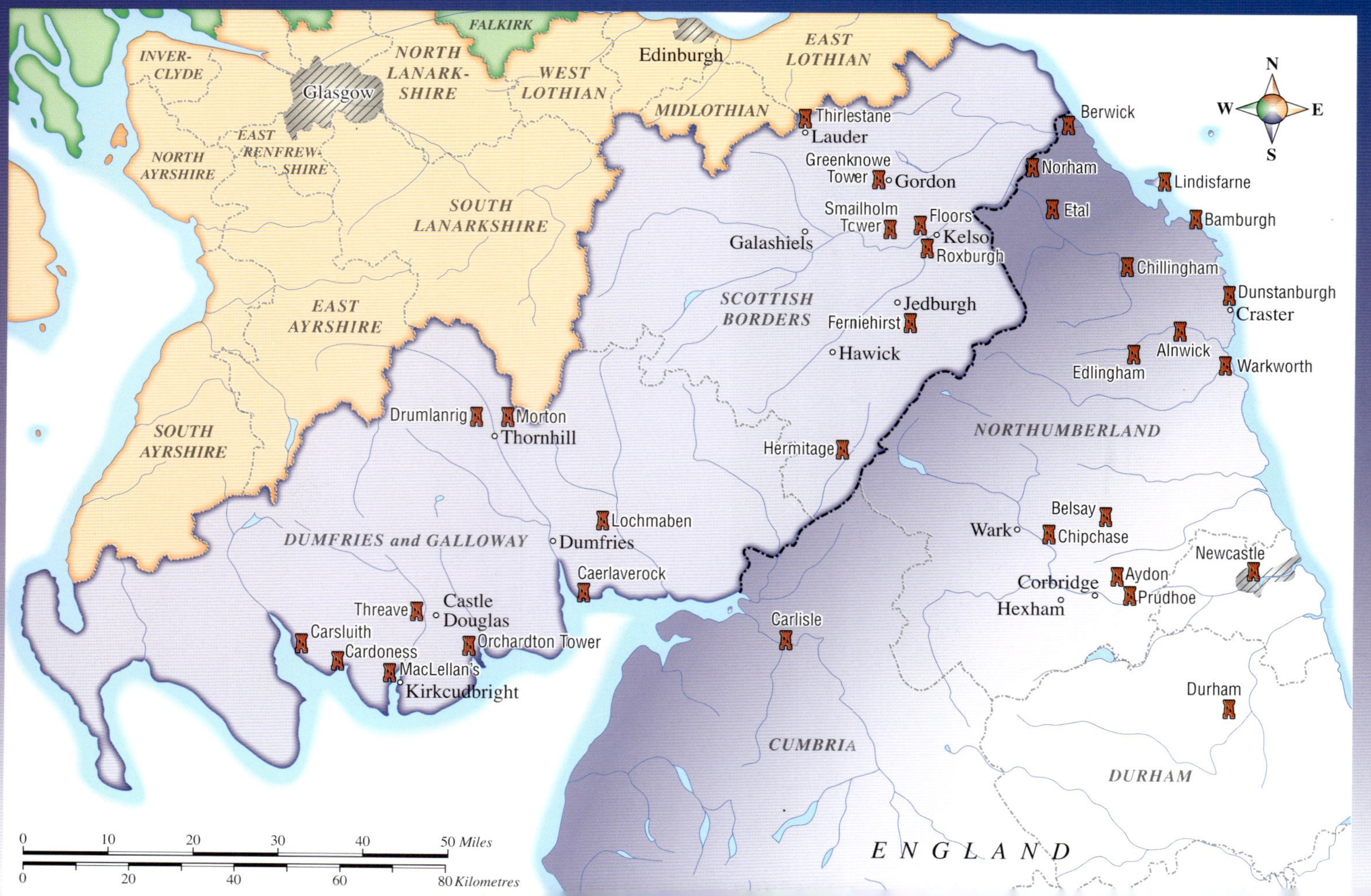

INVER-CLYDE
NORTH AYRSHIRE
EAST RENFREW-SHIRE
NORTH LANARK-SHIRE
FALKIRK
WEST LOTHIAN
Edinburgh
EAST LOTHIAN
MIDLOTHIAN
Glasgow
SOUTH LANARKSHIRE
EAST AYRSHIRE
SOUTH AYRSHIRE
Thirlestane
Lauder
Greenknowe Tower
Gordon
Smailholm Tower
Floors
Kelso
Roxburgh
Galashiels
SCOTTISH BORDERS
Jedburgh
Ferniehirst
Hawick
Berwick
Norham
Etal
Lindisfarne
Bamburgh
Chillingham
Dunstanburgh
Craster
Alnwick
Warkworth
Edlingham
NORTHUMBERLAND
Drumlanrig
Morton
Thornhill
Hermitage
Lochmaben
DUMFRIES and GALLOWAY
Dumfries
Caerlaverock
Belsay
Wark
Chipchase
Newcastle
Corbridge
Aydon
Hexham
Prudhoe
Carlisle
Threave
Castle Douglas
Carsluith
Cardoness
Orchardton Tower
MacLellan's
Kirkcudbright
CUMBRIA
Durham
DURHAM
ENGLAND
N
W
E
S
0   10   20   30   40   50 Miles
0   20   40   60   80 Kilometres

Southern Scotland and the English Borders

Unlike the craggy mountains and barren moor lands of the Highlands, Scotland's southern uplands feature a more gentle landscape of grassy undulating hills. The Tweed Valley is the gateway to England and territories here, both north and south of the border, were fiercely fought over. The Scots built massive strongholds, such as Caerlaverock and Roxburgh, while powerful families in the north of England built mighty fortresses to defend their lands in England.

Location: *Northumberland*

Map ref: *NU 187137*

Tel: *01665 510777 or 01665 511100 (24hrs)*

Web: *www.alnwickcastle.com*

Open: *Daily 10am–6pm (state rooms 11am–5pm) Apr–late Oct*

Alnwick

One of the best-known castles in Britain, its current popularity partly attributable to its starring role in the *Harry Potter* films, Alnwick's history is as interesting as any work of fiction. The castle is still the seat of the Dukes of Northumberland and is the second-largest inhabited castle in the country.

History

Yves de Vescy built the earliest parts of the fortress in 1096 and by the middle of the 12th century the castle had taken on the basic plan that remains today. It was one of the earliest Norman fortresses to have been built without a square keep, and fragments of the Norman masonry still exist in the curtain walls.

The de Vescys held Alnwick through several sieges and periods of turbulence (Eustace de Vescy was a ringleader of the Barons' Revolt – the castle was ordered to be destroyed, but this wasn't carried out) until early in the 14th century when the fortress and manors of Alnwick were handed to Anthony Bek, Bishop of Durham. The direct male line of the de Vescys died out in 1314 at the Battle of Bannockburn and the Percy family, who became one of England's most powerful dynasties, came to Alnwick in 1309.

The Percys

The Percys were already important English landowners when Henry de Percy bought the castle. Henry, the 1st Lord Percy of Alnwick, started to transform the castle into a formidable stronghold and palatial residence – he reconstructed the keep and rebuilt most of the towers on the curtain wall. His son continued the reconstruction – the octagonal towers on either side of the keep's entrance are his and date from *c.*1350. Generations of Percys made their mark on Alnwick but during the second half of the 18th century Robert Adam altered the castle in the Gothic Revival style (much of this work was later removed). Around the same time Alnwick first became home to the Dukes of Northumberland.

The Percy family and Alnwick were often intertwined with many of the pivotal events of British history. Contemporary invaders of Alnwick are the visitors who come to view this important part of the nation's heritage and to be reminded of the ancestry of the present 12th Duke of Northumberland, Ralph Percy.

Today

Today the castle receives around 300,000 visitors per year and is becoming recognized as a must-see destination, both nationally and internationally. There certainly is plenty here to occupy visitors of all ages. The *Harry Potter* link will engage many children and, one day a week in the summer, Hagrid and Professor Dumbledore are on hand to perform magic. The Knight's School allows youngsters to experience what it was like to train as a knight. Also in summer a magician performs tricks and birds of prey are demonstrated. Alnwick's website offers lots of games and fun for children. If you feel like a break for refreshments, there is a tearoom.

The castle is filled with treasures, including paintings by celebrated artists such as Bellini, Gainsborough and Claude Lorraine, furniture and statues accumulated by the family and it has its own museum. Events are staged regularly and there are permanent displays to further your knowledge about the castle and the part it played in history.

The Alnwick Garden

Outside, the Duchess has supervised the transformation of an area of disused land into the Alnwick Garden, a reason for a visit in its own right. The garden, a charity, operates separately from the castle; for information, visit its website, www.alnwickgarden.com.

Location: *Near Corbridge, Northumberland*

Map ref: *NZ 001663*

Tel: *01434 632450*

Web: *www.english-heritage.org.uk*

Open: *Daily 10am–6pm late Mar–Sep*

Aydon

A wealthy Suffolk merchant built this fine example of a 13th-century manor house. Aydon was originally intended to be an undefended dwelling but was fortified early in the 14th century when disputes over border territories worsened. The castle was attacked by the Scots twice, in 1315 and again in 1346.

From the 17th century until the 1960s the castle was used as a farm but it has now been restored to its original medieval appearance.

For the visitor

Substantial parts of the original work survive and visitors can walk through the Great Hall, chambers, service rooms, kitchen and servants' accommodation, seeing them just as they would have been in medieval times. Refreshments are available.

Location: *Northumberland*

Map ref: *NZ 088785*

Tel: *01661 881636*

Web: *www.english-heritage.org.uk*

Open: *Daily 10am–5pm (4pm in Oct) Apr–Oct; Wed–Mon (closed Tue) 10am–4pm Nov–Mar*

Belsay

Belsay is a substantial stone tower house built during a period of turbulence in the borders. Although the castle was enlarged into a mansion in the 17th century, the 14th-century tower remains one of the best surviving examples of a 'pele' tower in England and the chamber on the first floor has traces of elaborate medieval wall paintings, giving the visitor an idea of early 'interior decoration' techniques. The castle's role, as a residence for the Middleton family, ended when it was replaced early in the 19th century by nearby Belsay Hall, an austere Greek Revival-style mansion with a stunning two-storey central Pillar Hall.

Gardens and grounds

Magnificent gardens link the two buildings and make for an enjoyable walk between the classical hall and medieval castle. A rugged and unusual quarry garden has been created where the stone was cut for the construction of the hall. Belsay has a shop and tearoom and the grounds are a good spot for a picnic. Events, usually family orientated, are held throughout the year – check the English Heritage website for details.

Berwick

Berwick Castle, first mentioned in documents dating from the 12th century, was once the most important of the border castles, a mighty fortress and a key objective for both the English and the Scottish armies – there are few castles that have changed hands so frequently. Edward I strengthened the castle and town walls after he seized Berwick in 1296 (Edward's army killed most of the town's population – the King was known as 'The Hammer of the Scots') but little is left of this once proud fortress; its scant remnants stand near the town's Victorian railway station. However Berwick does still have the most complete and impressive bastioned town defences in England, which date mainly from the Elizabethan era and the whole circuit can be walked.

Location: *Berwick-upon-Tweed, Northumberland*

Map ref: *NT 994535*

Tel: *0870 333 1181*

Web: *www.english-heritage.org.uk*

Open: Ramparts: *any reasonable time*

Location: *Dumfries & Galloway*

Map ref: *NT 025656*

Tel: *01387 770244*

Web: *www.historic-scotland.gov.uk*

Open: *Daily 9.30am–6.30pm Apr–Sep; daily 9.30am–4.30pm Oct–Mar*

Caerlaverock

'Caerlaverock was so strong a castle that it feared no siege … it had but three sides round it, with a tower at each corner but one of them was a double one, so high, so long and so wide, that the gate was underneath it, well made and strong, with a drawbridge and a sufficiency of other defences'. This is a translation of *Le Siège de Karlaverock*, a contemporary French rhyming account of Edward I's siege in 1300.

The castle was built *c*.1280–1300 and held by the English for 12 years. The constable then declared for Robert Bruce, dismantling the castle as required by the Scottish King.

Caerlaverock was rebuilt in the 15th century, following the original design – the massive gatehouse was strengthened and made residential. Gun-ports were inserted into the stonework for cannons and other small guns towards the end of the 16th century. In 1630 Lord Nithsdale built a three-storey residential block against the inner eastern wall. The castle was defended for the King against the Covenanters in 1640. The ruins retain much of the formidable defensive building work.

Visitor attractions

Visitors can see an exhibition on sieges or take a nature trail and there is an adventure playground for children. A café provides refreshments.

Location: *Northumberland*

Map ref: *NU 184351*

Tel: *01668 214515*

Web: *www.bamburghcastle.com*

Open: *Daily 11am–5pm mid-Mar–Oct. Last entry 30 mins before closing*

Bamburgh

Bamburgh, built by the Norman invaders in the 11th century, was an impregnable fortress and royal stronghold for around 400 years. In 1464, during the Wars of the Roses, this Lancastrian stronghold was the first English castle to fall to artillery ranged against it by the army of Edward IV. The earliest of the many sieges and skirmishes at the fortress came in 1095 when William II attacked Bamburgh using a siege castle nicknamed Malvoisin (Evil Neighbour) – the holder, Robert de Mowbray, was imprisoned for conspiring against the King, and from then until the early 17th century, Bamburgh remained for the most part in royal hands, maintained as a fortress crucially sited for defence against Scottish invaders. Its great keep is attributed to Henry II and the fortress hosted many visits by the English monarchs.

The castle's structure

The castle's formidable outline is still silhouetted against the skyline, much as it would have been when it was one of the most important northern strongholds. Its current grandeur owes more to the 18th and 19th centuries. Bamburgh was ruinous by the end of the 1600s

with only the keep remaining intact. The 1st Lord Armstrong, a noteworthy industrialist,
shipbuilder and engineer, purchased the property towards the end of the Victorian era,
and he began massive reconstruction and restoration at the fortress.

Early history

Bamburgh's origins go far beyond the Norman castle. A British tribe owned the site in the
1st century BC. Then the Romans established a citadel here, and when they left Britain there
is evidence that Bamburgh became the stronghold of a local chieftain. In AD547 Bamburgh
was the seat of the Anglo-Saxon King Ida. During the 7th century it came into the hands
of Edwin of Northumbria, who brought the Roman missionary Paulinus to preach around
Bamburgh. After Edwin's death, Oswald, the son of Edwin's adversary Ethelfrith, took
Bamburgh and established a monastery on Lindisfarne (Holy Island) in 625; this became
one of the world's great centres of learning, art and Christianity.

Museums

The castle houses two museums in the former laundry. The Armstrong Museum is dedicated
to the life and work of the 1st Lord Armstrong while the Bamburgh Castle Aviation Artefacts
Museum has aircraft from the 20th century, most notably from both World Wars.

Location: *Gatehouse of Fleet, Dumfries & Galloway*

Map ref: *NX 590522*

Tel: *01557 814427*

Web: *www.historic-scotland.gov.uk*

Open: *Daily 9.30am–6.30pm Apr–Sep; Sat–Wed 9.30am–4.30pm Oct; Sat & Sun 9.30am–4.30pm Nov–Mar*

Cardoness

The ruins of Cardoness stand on a rocky platform overlooking the Water of Fleet. The principal feature of the site is a well-preserved six-storey tower dating from the 15th century, which has both wide-mouthed and keyhole gun-ports as part of its defences. The basement is vaulted (it would have been divided in two by a floor to give extra storage) and there are some fine stone carvings and a fireplace to be explored in the Great Hall. Cardoness was built for the McCulloch family – it was abandoned at the end of the 17th century after Sir Godfrey McCulloch was executed for murdering a member of a rival family.

Visiting

Before heading up to the tower it is worth calling into the Visitor Centre to view a model of how the castle looked originally. The remains are substantial and there is a good deal to enjoy, not least the superb view. A steep path and six flights of steps lead up to the monument where an interpretive panel explains more of the castle's history and there are benches to rest on. Cardoness is not accessible for wheelchair users or recommended for visitors with mobility/breathing problems, although the shop and Visitor Centre at the foot of the hill are accessible.

Carlisle

The earliest castle structure at Carlisle was a wooden, palisaded enclosure, raised by William Rufus *c.*1092 on the high bluff overlooking the River Eden. Henry I is then recorded as having ordered a 'castle and towers' to be raised to fortify the city in 1122 and the first stone buildings were begun. The massive great tower was built later in the same century and is the oldest surviving part of the fortress.

Location: *Cumbria*

Map ref: *NY 396562*

Tel: *01228 591992*

Web: *www.english-heritage.org.uk*

Open: *Daily 9.30am–6pm Apr–Sep; daily 10am–4pm Oct–Mar*

Conflict and war

David I of Scotland seized Carlisle Castle but Henry II reclaimed the castle in 1157. Its position, at the western end of the border with Scotland, ensured that this fortress was a frequent scene of conflict and change of ownership. Edward I renovated Carlisle and used it as his seat of Government and headquarters when he invaded Scotland. Mary, Queen of Scots was held prisoner here following her abdication from the Scottish throne and the castle was also subjected to an eight-month siege when it was held by the Royalists during the Civil War. In 1746, the final time Carlisle was involved in clashes, supporters of 'Bonnie Prince Charlie' had to defend the castle against the Hanoverian army.

History

In the keep, a room that was used as a prison during the Jacobite Uprising has the 'licking stones', so called because prisoners were driven by thirst to lick the stones to try to get some moisture from them. Carlisle continued to be used as barracks late into the 20th century and houses the museum of the King's Own Royal Border Regiment and much else of interest. The Carlisle Roman Dig, also on the site, is an exhibition with objects from recent excavations. Events are held in the grounds.

Location: *Near Creetown, Dumfries & Galloway*

Map ref: *NX 494541*

Tel: *0131 668 8800*

Web: *www.historic-scotland.gov.uk*

Open: *Daily 9.30am–6.30pm Apr–Sep; daily 9.30am–4.30pm Oct–Mar*

Carsluith

Carsluith is an L-plan tower house dating from the 16th century and standing on a promontory overlooking Wigtown Bay. One of Carsluith's owners was the last Abbot of the Cistercian Sweetheart Abbey, which was founded in the memory of John Balliol by his widow, Lady Devorgilla. Other buildings on the castle site date from the 18th century.

No flooring or roofing remains above first floor level but a modern timber walkway has been constructed at roof level with views through the castle and the surrounding countryside – from here it is possible to get a sense of Carsluith's role as essentially a fortified domestic residence, the focus of a small settlement, rather than a formidable stronghold. Admission is free and there is a café on the site.

Chillingham

A licence to crenellate Chillingham was granted in 1344. What was little more than a single tower built in the previous century became an extensive but compact quadrangular castle with square-angle towers, and a curtain, of which there are scant remains.

Location: *Northumberland*

Map ref: *NU 061257*

Tel: *01668 215359*

Web: *www.chillingham-castle.com*

Open: Castle: *Sun–Fri (closed Sat) 1pm–5pm (last entry 4.30pm) Easter & May–Sep;* **Grounds and Tearoom:** *Sun–Fri (closed Sat) 12pm–5pm Easter & May–Sep*

A haunted castle

Somewhat altered over the centuries and the subject of wide-ranging restoration by its present occupants, Chillingham is, nevertheless, a fine example of a medieval castle with Tudor additions, and is still the family home of descendants of the original owners. The castle came under attack in 1536 and suffered some damage during the Pilgrimage of Grace rebellion but was successfully defended. Chillingham has the reputation of being one of the most haunted castles in England.

Restoration and renovation

In the 16th century the main entrance was repositioned in preparation for a visit by James VI of Scotland. Further alterations were carried out in the 18th and 19th centuries.

Rooms in the castle have been renovated to their original splendour. The state rooms have silk-screened walls and there is a restored Elizabethan ceiling in the James I Drawing Room. The Edward I Room is the oldest in the castle and has been re-created to its 13th-century style with furniture and armour. Paintings of monarchs are displayed in the Great Hall alongside tapestries, weapons and armour. The dungeons and torture chamber with their ranges of items once used to extract information might frighten younger children.

Chipchase

Chipchase sits on the western bank of the North Tyne. The fortified part is principally the 14th-century rectangular tower, which is at one end of the later 17th-century mansion. Further additions were made in the early part of the 19th century. Chipchase is a private family home and only open to the public for one month of the year but is one of the finest examples of Jacobean architecture in the country and can be viewed from outside when the castle grounds are open to visitors. The castle is set in 1.2 hectares (3 acres) of formal gardens and grounds and there is a specialist plant nursery operating out of the walled garden.

Location: *Wark, Hexham, Northumberland*

Map ref: *NY 882758*

Tel: *01434 230203*

Web: *www.chipchaseplants.co.uk*

Open: Castle: *daily 2pm–5pm 1–28 Jun;* **Gardens:** *Thu–Sun & Bank Holidays 10am–5pm Apr–Jul;* **Nursery:** *Thu–Sun & Bank Holidays 10am–5pm Apr–mid-Oct*

Location: *Thornhill, Dumfries & Galloway*

Map ref: *NX 851989*

Tel: *01848 600 283*

Web: *www.drumlanrig.com*

Open: Castle and Tearoom: *daily 12pm–4pm May–Jun; daily 11am–4pm Jul–Aug;* **Gardens and Country Park:** *daily 11am–5pm Apr–Sep*

Drumlanrig

Drumlanrig – known as 'The Pink Palace' – is a fine example of a late 17th-century Renaissance mansion and was built on the site of an ancient Douglas stronghold. The Douglas's have been associated with the castle since the 14th century.

The castle houses one of the finest private art collections in the country including paintings by Rembrandt, Holbein and Gainsborough. A famous Da Vinci work, 'Madonna with the Yarnwinder', was stolen from the castle in 2003 and has never been recovered. The castle can be viewed only by guided tour, where visitors can see the bedroom that 'Bonnie Prince Charlie' occupied in 1745 on his retreat northwards, and some of his personal relics.

Things to do

The castle gardens are outstanding, particularly the East Parterre, planted to an original 18th-century design, the Shawl Garden, the quaint Heather Houses (constructed as summer houses around the estate in the 1840s) and the breathtaking vista of the Great Avenue.

The Country Park offers cycling (there are bikes for hire at the castle) and way-marked walking. Children will enjoy the woodland adventure playground and watching pictures from the wildlife cameras in the Visitor Centre. Craft and art studios, a cycle museum and birds of prey demonstrations are further attractions. Refreshment can be found in the castle tearoom.

Dunstanburgh

Dunstanburgh was a lavish stonework enclosure castle whose main feature was the huge gatehouse tower at the southern end. The first buildings were erected in the early 14th century and included the massive three-storey gatehouse, with its cylindrical towers rising another two storeys. Now in ruins, the gatehouse contained a Great Hall on the second floor, with tall, mullioned and transomed windows positioned at each end.

Location: *Near Craster, Northumberland*

Map ref: *NU 258220*

Tel: *01665 576231 (Custodian)*

Web: *www.nationaltrust.org.uk*

Open: *Daily 10am–6pm Apr–Sep; daily 1pm–4pm Oct; Thu–Mon 10am–4pm Nov–Mar*

A Lancastrian stronghold

Built by Thomas, Earl of Lancaster who opposed Edward II for his bad Government and his infelicitous choice of friends (particularly Piers Gaveston), Dunstanburgh passed in due course to John of Gaunt. In the 1370s and 1380s Gaunt closed up the entrance to the gatehouse with a stone wall and a forebuilding (now disappeared) and turned it into a residential great tower, building an alternative gateway with a barbican. Dunstanburgh, a Lancastrian stronghold, was besieged during the Wars of the Roses and suffered much damage from the Yorkist cannons.

Dunstanburgh is now an impressive ruin standing high on the cliffs above the sea.

Durham

The site of Durham started as a motte castle, erected in a loop of the River Wear granted to the Prince-bishop of Durham in 1072. The chapel of 1080 still survives.

The Bishop's Palace

In the early 12th century a shell enclosure of sandstone in a roughly octagonal plan was erected on the motte around the wooden tower and this may have remained for some time; the shell was destroyed in 1340 and rebuilt. Domestic buildings were added within the banked, ditched and partly curtained bailey, including a range to the north, a 13th- to 14th-century Great Hall, a gatehouse and a kitchen. Although primarily a Bishop's Palace rather than a fortress, the castle was always kept ready for defence. Prince-bishops were expected to levy an army in times of threat, in return for absolute power over their bishopric.

Location: *County Durham*

Map ref: *NZ 273423*

Tel: *0191 334 3800 (Porter)*

Web: *www.durhamcastle.com*

Open: *Daily Easter–Sep, guided tours only*

The University

The keep was rebuilt in the middle of the 19th century when the castle became the site of Durham University but the Great Hall, used as the dining hall of University College, is medieval. It was first built by Bishop Anthony Bek (1284–1311) and then altered by Bishop Thomas Hatfield later in the 14th century. The walls of the palace-castle were connected with the city's walls, and the entire peninsula was enclosed by the river, with the magnificent cathedral included.

Together with the cathedral, the castle at Durham has been declared a UNESCO World Heritage Site.

Location: *Near Alnwick, Northumberland*

Map ref: *NU 116092*

Tel: *0870 333 1181*

Web: *www.english-heritage.org.uk*

Open: *Open access at any reasonable time*

Edlingham

A picturesque but very ruinous castle, Edlingham is set in a ruggedly attractive valley, which is the main draw for visitors. The castle was first begun at the end of the 13th century when a long rectangular hall in a moated enclosure was built; then a gatehouse, a small tower/keep and curtain wall were added. By the middle of the 17th century the castle was abandoned and a great deal of stone had been removed for other buildings. The ruins date from the 13th–14th centuries.

There are no facilities at the castle site but there is a small car park.

Location: *Northumberland*

Map ref: *NT 925393*

Tel: *01890 820332*

Web: *www.english-heritage.org.uk*

Open: *Daily 11am–4pm Apr–Oct*

Etal

In 1341 Robert Manners was granted permission to fortify his three-storey tower house which was sited in a strategic and vulnerable position by a ford over the River Till. He created a square courtyard castle enclosed by curtain walls. The tower house was improved with the addition of another storey and crenellations. Etal Castle which was, by then, in the care of a constable, fell to the army of James IV during his invasion of England in 1513 but the Scots were defeated soon after at the nearby Battle of Flodden Field. After the Union of the English and Scottish Crowns early in the 17th century, the castle lost its strategic importance.

Award-winning exhibition

Although Etal Castle is fairly ruinous, an award-winning exhibition about the Battle of Flodden Field and border warfare on the site makes a visit well worthwhile. There is a shop and it is also possible to picnic in the grounds.

Ferniehirst

Ferniehirst is known as 'Scotland's Frontier Fortress' owing to its position just inside the Anglo-Scottish border. It is mainly a 16th-century reconstruction of an earlier building and was seized by the forces of Henry III in 1547. For much of the 20th century the castle was used as a youth hostel, but it is once again a private home and has been lovingly restored.

Location: *Jedburgh, Scottish Borders*

Map ref: *NT 632179*

Tel: *01835 862201*

Web: *www.ferniehirst.com*

Open: *Tue–Sun 11am–4pm Jul only*

Visiting the castle

Highlights of this castle, which is only open for one month of the year (or by appointment at other times), include the Hall of History – a series of friezes that tell the story of the construction of the castle and some of its pivotal events – and the Turret Library. There is a small museum in one of the oldest parts of the castle and the Visitors Centre, located in a nearby 17th-century building and open when the castle is open, displays more information and a model of this pretty fortress. Visitors lucky enough to view its enchanting interior will get a glimpse inside a castle that is still entirely used as an ancestral family home.

There is also a pleasant walk along Jed Water and through Ferniehirst Wood to enjoy.

Floors

Floors Castle overlooks the Cheviot Hills and in front of it is the River Tweed – on the opposite bank are the ruins of Roxburgh Castle (page 117). Floors is the largest inhabited castle in Scotland, and is the home of the Duke and Duchess of Roxburghe.

In 1721 the 1st Duke of Roxburghe commissioned William Adam to add to an existing tower house on the site to create a fairly plain Georgian country house. Then, in 1837, the 6th Duke asked Edinburgh's leading architect, William Playfair, to remodel the residence and Floors became the romantic fairytale castle it is today.

Location: *Kelso, Scottish Borders*

Map ref: *NT 711347*

Tel: *01573 223333*

Web: *www.floorscastle.com*

Open: **Castle:** *daily 11am–5pm Easter & May–end Oct;* **Coffee Shop & Garden Centre:** *daily all year 9.30am–5pm*

Duchess May

The castle interiors are largely influenced by the flair of the American wife of the 8th Duke, Duchess May who had many of the rooms refitted in the first half of the 20th century and numerous treasures on display in the castle were collected by her. A full-length portrait of Duchess May by Edward Hughes can be viewed in the Billiard Room. The Roxburghe Coronation Robes and part of the family's costume collection are displayed in the Robe Room, which was once used as a laboratory by the 6th Duke who had a great interest in science. His collection of birds in the Bird Room may amuse young visitors.

Gardens and grounds

In the parkland in front of the house is a holly tree that marks the spot where James II of Scotland was killed by his own cannon as he besieged Roxburgh Castle in 1460. The walled garden, where Queen Victoria took tea on her visit in 1867, is to the west of the castle. Children will enjoy the adventure playground, while adults may prefer the garden centre and café or restaurant. Other attractions include the Star Plantation Woodland, the Millennium Parterre and way-marked woodland and riverside walks (dogs are welcome in the grounds). The shop in the café sells a range of home-produced food goodies. Visitors using wheelchairs are well catered for and information is enthusiastically offered by a team of friendly, knowledgeable guides. Events at the castle are posted on the website.

<table>
<tr><td>

Location: *Gordon, Scottish Borders*

Map ref: *NT 639428*

Tel: *0131 668 8800*

Web: *www.historic-scotland.gov.uk*

Open: *Open access*

</td></tr>
</table>

Greenknowe Tower

Greenknowe is a handsome and interesting L-plan tower house, built in 1581 by the Seton of Touch family. The lintel above the doorway has the date of construction and the initials of James Seton and his wife. It was occupied until the middle of the 19th century; the entrance is still guarded by its iron yett. Externally the tower ruins are fairly complete, inside though they are open to the elements above the first floor hall. There is a viewing platform in the stair wing, which is a pleasant place to admire the surrounding countryside. Greenknowe is not one of the best visitor attractions in Scotland, by any stretch of the imagination, but it is an interesting focal point for a pleasant walk – the path from the road is up a gentle incline. Parts of the surface of the courtyard that once surrounded the tower are still visible. There is an interpretive panel at the site.

Hermitage

This brutal-looking tower-house castle, set against a backdrop of bleak moorland, was built over several centuries. Its position meant that it figured in many episodes of Scottish history and it changed hands several times, particularly during the Wars of Independence in the 13th and 14th centuries. For a time Hermitage Castle was held by the wild and dangerous James Hepburn, Earl of Bothwell, whose liaison with Mary, Queen of Scots was the scandal of 16th-century Scotland.

History

The castle was begun in the early 13th century when Sir Nicholas de Soules put up a wooden fortress, which was captured in 1338 by the Knight of Liddesdale, Sir William Douglas. The 1st Earl of Douglas inherited Hermitage and built the original stone structure, a small rectangular enclosure, in the late 13th to early 14th centuries. Four great stone towers were added at the end of the 14th century: these are close together on the east and west sides and linked at the top by a continuous storey, giving the appearance of a huge stone wall with a great central pointed arch, reaching to the top storey from the ground. There were more alterations, notably the provision of wide-mouth gun-ports in the 1540s.

The castle fell into disuse in the 1600s but its reputation as a forbidding ruin endured. Famously, Sir Walter Scott was painted with Hermitage Castle in the background in the 19th century. Although the exterior walls are largely intact, the interior is in a ruinous state. It is widely believed by local people that the castle is haunted by ghosts.

<table>
<tr><td>

Location: *Scottish Borders*

Map ref: *NY 497961*

Tel: *01387 372622*

Web: *www.historic-scotland.gov.uk*

Open: *Mon–Sat 9.30am–6.30pm, Sun 2pm–6.30pm Apr–Sep*

</td></tr>
</table>

Lindisfarne

Lindisfarne Castle dates from the 16th century – it was built to defend a harbour that sheltered English ships at war with Scotland. Holy Island is usually associated with the ancient monastic community that became one of the most important centres of Christianity in Anglo-Saxon England, and it is also remembered as the location of the first attack on Britain's coastline by Scandinavian Vikings. Despite its volatile location, the Tudor fortress remained unscathed and lost its importance with the Union of the Crowns, but a garrison remained at the castle until late in the 19th century.

Location: *Holy Island, Northumberland*

Map ref: *NU 136417*

Tel: *01289 389244*

Web: *www.nationaltrust.org.uk*

Open: *Feb half-term & mid-Mar–end Oct and occasional days between Christmas and New Year. Times vary according to tides – please telephone the castle for details. The National Trust flag flies only when the castle is open.*
Garden: *daily all year 10am–dusk*

Lindisfarne and Lutyens

What helps make Lindisfarne especially interesting to visitors today are the Lutyens interiors and the walled garden, which was planted by the influential garden designer, Gertrude Jekyll. The castle's owner, and the founder of *Country Life* magazine, Edward Hudson commissioned Sir Edwin Lutyens to remodel the castle into a comfortable residence. Lutyens' upturned boat hulls as garden sheds are an amusing feature in the castle grounds. The castle is perched on top of the highest point of the island and has wonderful views across the sea to the formidable outline of the mighty stronghold of Bamburgh Castle (page 100) and the Farne Islands. Visitors with mobility problems may find the steep slopes, steps and uneven floors difficult to negotiate. Holy Island is only accessible (by vehicle or on foot) via the causeway, which runs from the mainland – this is closed from two hours before high tide until three hours after. Tide times are posted on the causeway and at the castle – they are also available at www.lindisfarne.org.uk.

<table>
<tr><td>

Location: *Dumfries & Galloway*

Map ref: *NY 088811*

Tel: *0131 668 8800*

Web: *www.historic-scotland.gov.uk*

Open: *Open access*

</td></tr>
</table>

Lochmaben

There have been two Lochmaben castles. The first was built by the Bruce family as a motte castle in the 1160s and given stonework by the time the castle was captured by Edward I late in the 13th century. Edward built a new castle in a more strategic position and all that remains of the first Lochmaben is the motte. Edward's substantial new castle, which played a significant role in the Wars of Independence, was a complex design with a 'canal' running between the inner and outer wards. The castle was extensively rebuilt during the reign of James IV but then dismantled after its capture by James VI in 1588. Lochmaben is very ruinous but the site has some interesting detail and an interpretive panel. There are good views across Castle Loch, and there are picnic tables and benches at the site.

MacLellan's

MacLellan's Castle, which could be described as a 'borderline' castle, was a grand, noble residence built on the L-plan in 1582 by Sir Thomas MacLellan Provost of Kirkcudbright. It was constructed from the stones of an old convent of the Greyfriars that stood on the site and which had become derelict after the Reformation. Built for show rather than defence, MacLellan's was a mix of fortified castle (minimum window space in the lower storeys, no direct access between the basement and the hall, and a spy-hole, which doubtless could be used as a shot-hole) and a spacious, comfortable residence. The castle was stripped of its roof and contents in the 18th century.

<table>
<tr><td>

Location: *Kirkcudbright, Dumfries & Galloway*

Map ref: *NX 682510*

Tel: *01557 331856*

Web: *www.historic-scotland.gov.uk*

Open: *Daily 9.30am–6.30pm Apr–Sep*

</td></tr>
</table>

The shell of MacLellan's castle stands, largely complete, in the centre of Kirkcudbright. The castle itself is not accessible to wheelchair users but there is an interpretive panel in the grounds. There is an admission charge and a small shop.

Location: *Near Carronbridge, Dumfries & Galloway*

Map ref: *NX 891992*

Tel: *0131 668 8800*

Web: *www.historic-scotland.gov.uk*

Open: *Open access at any reasonable time*

Morton

Not much remains of this rectangular hall-tower, which was once a Douglas stronghold and part of a chain of castles along the Nith Valley (running from the Solway Firth to the Clyde Valley). Morton was one of the fortresses mentioned in the Treaty of Berwick (1357) that secured the release of David II from imprisonment by Edward III, but required the destruction of 13 castles in Nithsdale. The castle was then rebuilt in the 15th century. It was occupied until the start of the 18th century (at least in part) and then fell into dereliction – remnants of two of its towers still stand. Morton's design bears a resemblance to Caerlaverock (page 99). The castle is owned by the Duke of Buccleuch but is in the care of Historic Scotland.

A spectacular location

It is the spectacular location that really earns Morton's remnants a place in this book. On a high, triangular promontory, overlooking Morton Loch and the Lowther Hills on the far side, they stand in one of the most breathtaking settings of any Scottish fortress and there can be few better places to take a walk and have a picnic. The loch was created in the 18th century when a dam was built to flood the surrounding marshland and which now surrounds the castle on three sides, but this has only enhanced the attraction of this romantic ruin. It was the setting for some of the scenes in the 1978 version of *The Thirty-Nine Steps* starring Robert Powell.

Access to the castle from the main road is via a gated pathway. There are no direction signs until you are quite close and wheelchair access is difficult.

Newcastle

Newcastle began as a motte castle with a bank and ditch, built by Robert Curthose, William the Conqueror's eldest son, in 1080. During the late 11th and early 12th centuries ownership of the northern counties of England was disputed with Scotland and for a time Newcastle was held by the Scottish Kings.

Location: *Tyne and Wear*

Map ref: *NZ 250638*

Tel: *0191 2327938*

Web: *http://museums.ncl.ac.uk/ keep/*

Open: *Daily 9.30am–5.30pm Apr–Sep; daily 9.30am–4.30pm Oct–Mar*

The great tower

A new stone castle was begun by Henry II in 1168. Work continued for about ten years under Mauricius Caementarius (Maurice the Engineer), and included a substantial rectangular great tower within a curtain wall. The great tower with its vaulted basement was restored in the mid-19th century and now houses a museum. It is one of the best surviving examples of a Norman keep in the country.

History

The curtain enclosure was many sided, with postern gates and rectangular flanking towers. Additional buildings raised against the inside in later years include the aisled Great Hall of *c.*1210, which was dismantled in 1809. In 1247–50 a tower gatehouse, the Black Gate, which survives, was added to the more vulnerable western edge of the castle site. Once the town walls were completed in the middle of the 14th century, the castle's defensive significance declined. It was garrisoned again briefly during the Civil War.

Visiting the castle

Visitors can climb a spiral staircase to the restored battlements for good views. The keep and Black Gate are both open and have many areas of interest. The website includes an excellent virtual tour.

Norham

Norham, founded *c*.1120, was sited at a strategic crossing point of the south bank of the River Tweed. The first castle here was destroyed by the Scots but rebuilt in stone in the 1160s on the orders of Henry II – the great tower was built at this time.

The most dangerous place in the country

Norham was besieged at least 13 times – it gained a reputation for being 'the most dangerous and adventurous place in the country'. The Scots employed the famous siege gun Mons Meg (now on display at Edinburgh Castle) during one attack. In 1513, James IV besieged, captured and virtually destroyed the fortress but following the defeat of the Scots at the Battle of Flodden Field, the castle was returned to the English. In the 19th century the ruins became a favourite subject of the Romantic artist JMW Turner.

Location: *Near Berwick-upon-Tweed, Northumberland*

Map ref: *NT 906476*

Tel: *01289 304493*

Web: *www.english-heritage.org.uk*

Open: *Please telephone for opening hours. Grounds are freely accessible.*

For the visitor

There is plenty explore among the ruins when the castle is open (wheelchair users can access all but the keep). The mainly grassy castle grounds are perfect for picnics.

Location: *Near Dalbeattie, Dumfries & Galloway*

Map ref: *NX 817551*

Tel: *0131 668 8800*

Web: *www.historic-scotland.gov.uk*

Open: *Open access at any reasonable time*

Orchardton Tower

Orchardton is Scotland's only freestanding circular tower house. It was built in the 15th century and internal arrangements are much the same as those of a rectangular tower house. The entrance to the tower is at first-floor level accessed by an external stairway, and a very narrow spiral staircase inside is in the wall thickness. The top of the tower has a gabled cap-house resting on a corbelled parapet. It is possible to climb the staircase and enjoy the view of the surrounding countryside from the wall walk, or look down into the inside of the tower. The outbuildings belonging to this charming and surprisingly complete tower are ruinous, but they would have included a hall and service buildings such as a kitchen and brewhouse.

Wheelchair users will find it difficult to access the tower as a steep flight of steps leads up to the entrance. There is a good view of Orchardton from the car park.

Prudhoe

Prudhoe means 'proud heights' and is pronounced 'pruddah'. The castle is set on a wooded slope and was built between 1100 and 1120 to defend a strategic crossing on the River Tyne. Around 1175, after suffering two sieges, a mighty stone keep was built in the western part of the enclosure. The gatehouse was also built in the 12th century and in the very early 14th century a barbican was added, which led to a drawbridge across the moat. The gatehouse was given a vaulted basement and a chapel on the first floor, which is noted for its oriel window.

Location: *Northumberland*	
Map ref: *NZ 092634*	
Tel: *01661 833459*	
Web: *www.english-heritage.org.uk*	
Open: *Daily 10am–5pm Apr–Sep*	

Prudhoe was originally owned by the Umfravile family but came into the hands of the mighty Percy Earls of Northumberland, through marriage, at the end of the 14th century. The fortress saw its last military action against the Scots in 1640 but its importance as the centre of a great landed estate continued. Early in the 19th century the castle was restored, and the 2nd Duke of Northumberland (a Percy) built a manor house inside the walls. The seat of the Duke of Northumberland is at Alnwick Castle (page 96) although the family still own Prudhoe, however it is now managed by English Heritage.

For the visitor

The gatehouse and curtain wall are the best-preserved parts of the medieval castle – the keep is fairly ruinous but nevertheless adds to the fortress's formidable outline. Prudhoe's history is vividly interpreted in a new family-friendly exhibition, which includes site finds, displayed in the Georgian mansion house. There is also a video presentation on the story of Northumberland's castles and their role in the border wars. Picnics are welcome and there is a shop but no refreshments. Disabled drivers may park within the castle, in front of the house.

Roxburgh

Roxburgh is first recorded as the residence of the Earl of Northumberland in 1107 (when the castle was known as Marchidun). When Earl David became David I of Scotland he renamed the castle and Roxburgh came to the forefront of Scottish politics. At the height of its powers, the fortress was a massive construction with the burgh of Roxburgh to its east, rivalling Edinburgh or Berwick in importance.

Location: *Near Kelso, Scottish Borders*

Map ref: *NT 712337*

Tel: *01573 223333*

Web: *www.floorscastle.com (part of the Roxburghe estate)*

Open: *Open access*

An evocative site

Nothing now remains of the town and there are only fragments of the most important of the border fortresses on the grassy mound overlooking the Rivers Teviot and Tweed. The castle fell into English hands at the end of the 13th century but a daring assault by the infamous Black Douglas took back the castle for the Scots – the exploit was related by the poet John Barbour in his epic *The Bruce*. Despite the lack of remains it is still evocative to visit the shrubby mound of the castle's site where there are very fine views across to Floors Castle (page 109). Roxburgh lies on the path of the way-marked circular walking route – the Borders Abbeys Way.

Smailholm Tower

A favourite castle of Sir Walter Scott, Smailholm Tower is a four-floor rectangular tower house standing on a rocky spur surrounded on three sides by cliffs and enclosed by a ditch and stone walling. The tower walls are almost 3m (10ft) thick and the tower reaches nearly 18.5m (60ft). The castle, which was built by the Pringle family in the 15th century, is now decayed and a fairly substantial ruin.

Visitors will be able to admire the surrounding areas from the top of the tower house. The castle has a display of costumed dolls and tapestries.

Location: *Scottish Borders*

Map ref: *NT 638346*

Tel: *01573 460365*

Web: *www.historic-scotland. gov.uk*

Open: *Daily 9.30am–6.30pm Apr–Sep; Sat–Wed 9.30am–4.30pm Oct; Sat–Sun 9.30am–4.30pm Nov–Mar*

Location: *Lauder, Scottish Borders*

Map ref: *NT 533479*

Tel: *01578 722430*

Web: *www.thirlestanecastle.co.uk*

Open: *Hours change every year. 2007: 10am–3pm (last entry) Easter (Fri, Sun & Mon); Sun, Wed & Thu Apr–Jun; Sun–Thu Jul & Aug; Sun, Wed & Thu Sep; Special opening can be arranged. Tearoom: 10am–5pm on normal castle open days*

Thirlestane

Thirlestane stands at a vital strategic point en route to the centre of Scotland. There has been a fortification here for more than 700 years, guarding Edinburgh from southern invaders. The ruins of the old tower of Thirlestane are around 3.2km (2 miles) from the present fairytale castle, which is the result of three main periods of building in the 16th, 17th and 19th centuries.

It was the 1st Baron Maitland who began the construction – he left the old tower and at the end of the 16th century started to build the great stone keep at the heart of the present castle. His design was unusually symmetrical for its time, with four large drum towers at each corner, but it was essentially still a fortified tower house. Less than a hundred years later Sir William Bruce, the architect who changed the face of many of Scotland's great buildings, modified Thirlestane into a flamboyant Renaissance palace. When the grand Scottish estates were enjoying their social apogee under Queen Victoria in the 19th century, two large wings were added to accommodate the growing number of guests and their servants who came to Scotland for the summer grouse shooting parties and other grand social occasions. The architects, David Bryce and William Burns gave Thirlestane its spectacular skyline. They copied Bruce's designs in their additions, raised the central tower and added an ogee roof flanking it with a series of conical turrets.

The Maitland family

The Maitlands (or de Matulants) came from France with William the Conqueror and rose to prominence throughout the middle ages. Their first major family seat was Lethington (now Lennoxlove, page 90), which was home to Sir William Maitland, Secretary to Mary, Queen of Scots. His brother John served as Lord Chancellor to James VI and it was John who began the present Thirlestane Castle. John's grandson, the 1st and only Duke of Lauderdale, made the 17th-century alterations to transform the castle into a sumptuous residence, suitable for a member of Charles II's inner cabinet. His career ended ignominiously and, dying without an heir, all the titles conferred on him became extinct – his younger brother inherited the earldom of Lauderdale. After his death, the Duke's wife, Elizabeth, removed many of the castle's contents to Ham House in Richmond, her family home. The people of Lauder were incensed and prevented the last wagonload from leaving the estate.

Things to see

Visitors to Thirlestane can enjoy the splendour of the elaborate stuccoed ceilings that were commissioned in the 17th century, particularly in the Grand Bed Chamber. The castle combines Baroque grandeur with the atmosphere of a grand Victorian country house. A collection of Georgian, Edwardian and Victorian toys, games and children's clothes can be found in the old nurseries, and a glimpse into the working lives of the ghillies and gamekeepers, gardeners, farm workers and other country folk that have been employed on the Maitland estate from the 17th century is revealed in the Border Country Life exhibition.

Facilities

There is a tearoom and gift shop in the castle and children will love the adventure playground in the grounds, constructed on the site of an old artillery fort. Picnic tables are provided in a wooded area near the castle. Although disabled visitors can alight at the entrance to the castle, access for wheelchair users may be difficult – there is a flight of 22 steps to the door of the castle and the tour covers three floors and 87 steps. The tearoom is accessible.

Threave

Threave Castle stands on an islet in the River Dee and even as a ruin it is a mighty and forbidding structure. The massive great tower was partly enclosed by a powerful artillery wall, which had three cylindrical corner turrets.

Location: *Near Castle Douglas, Dumfries & Galloway*

Map ref: *NX 739623*

Tel: *07711 223101*

Web: *www.historic-scotland.gov.uk*

Open: *Daily 9.30am–6.30pm Apr–Sep*

Inspiring awe

Built by Archibald 'the Grim', 3rd Earl of Douglas, Lord of Galloway, in about 1370, Threave was a defensive structure as well as a building intended to impress. During the reign of James II, the Earls of Douglas were locked in a deadly quarrel with the King who was determined to break their power.

In *c.*1454, defences were reinforced with the addition of the earliest artillery wall in Britain along the sides of the castle that faced the mainland. The wall was 5.5m (18ft) tall and it was provided with vertical loops with embrasures for handguns and for crossbows – its towers were equipped with two types of gun-port, inverted keyholes and dumb-bells. Threave was besieged in 1455 by James II using the latest cannons and bombards, including the famous Mons Meg (now at Edinburgh Castle), and was eventually taken. It was slighted in the 17th century.

Visiting the castle

Today access to the islet is by taking a boat that departs from the small jetty standing nearby. The property is closed in winter. There is a walk of about 2km (1¼ miles) to the castle from the boat. You will find a tearoom next to the car park.

Warkworth

A late motte castle of the mid-12th century, Warkworth eventually developed into a masterpiece of late medieval architecture and was home to the most powerful family in the North. One part of the castle was ranged around the outer bailey and the

Location: *Northumberland*

Map ref: *NU 247058*

Tel: *01665 711423*

Web: *www.english-heritage.org.uk*

Open: *Daily 10am–5pm Apr–Sep; daily 10am–4pm Oct; Sat–Mon 10am–4pm Nov–Mar*

other was contained within a magnificent multi-angular keep. Henry, son of David I of Scotland, probably built the earliest castle but it was the English Clavering (or FitzRoger) family who built the great gateway and massive curtain with flanking towers.

Early plumbing

By the end of the 13th century the castle was visited by Edward I. Warkworth was granted to the Percys in 1332. The Percys built the polygonal Grey Mare's Tail Tower and much later in the 14th century the keep was erected – its apartments were grouped round a square lantern turret that ingeniously collected rainwater, channelled it to a tank in the basement and then distributed it to garderobes and basins. The keep is still a magnificent sight. The Percys remained at the castle until the Reformation when the castle was pillaged. In the 19th century Anthony Salvin carried out some restoration.

For the visitor

This is a wonderful castle to explore, many of the walls have gone but the remains allow you to imagine Warkworth when it was a place of power and wealth. Refreshments are available on the site.

Glossary

The following terms are used both in this book and more generally, to describe the distinctive architectural features of castles.

adulterine unlicensed castle

apse circular or polygonal end of a tower or chapel

arcading rows of arches supported on columns

arrow-loop or slit long, narrow (usually vertical) opening in wall or battlements. Round or triangular ends were for cross-bows, as were horizontal cross-slits which gave greater range

ashlar blocks of smooth, squared stone of any kind

bailey or ward courtyard within the castle walls

barbican outward defensive continuation of a gateway or entrance

barmkin, bawn yard surrounded by outer defensive walling

barrel vault semicircular roof (stone or timber)

bartizan small turret projecting from the corner or flank of a tower or wall, usually at the top

bastion tower or turret projecting from a wall or at the junction of two walls

battlements or crenellation the parapet of a tower or wall with indentations or openings (**embrasures** or **crenelles**) alternating with solid projections (**merlons**)

belfry tall moveable tower on wheels used in sieges

buttress projecting pillar added to strengthen a wall

corbel stone bracket projecting from a wall or corner

cross-wall internal dividing wall in a great tower

curtain general word for walling enclosing a courtyard. Sited between towers, or tower and gatehouse, and appearing to hang between them

donjon alternative name for a great tower

drawbridge wooden bridge (which could be raised and lowered) across a moat

dressing carved or smooth stonework around openings and along edges

forebuilding structure on the outside wall of a great tower protecting the entrance and all or part of the approaching stairs. Some forebuildings contained chambers and chapels over the stairs

gallery long narrow passage or room

garderobe latrine

gatehouse room over the castle entrance

great tower or keep the main tower of a castle

gun-loop or gun-port opening in a wall for a gun

hoarding defensive covered wooden gallery placed above a tower or curtain. Floor was slatted to allow defenders to drop missiles or liquids on to besiegers

jamb straight side of a doorway, archway or window

light windowpane or window division

lintel horizontal beam of wood or stone positioned across the top of an opening

machiolation projecting part of a stone or brick parapet with holes in the floor, as in hoarding

mangonel stone-throwing machine

meurtrière or murder hole opening in the roof or a gateway or part of gatehouse over an entrance. Popularly believed to be used in the same way as hoardings, but might have enabled defenders to channel water to wooden areas set on fire by attackers

motte a mound on which a castle was built (man-made or natural)

oriel window projecting curved or polygonal window

oubliette dungeon or pit reached by trap-door used for holding prisoners (in Scotland a **pit prison**)

palisade a defensive fence

pele tower small tower house

pilaster buttress buttress with a projection, positioned in corner or mid-wall

pipe rolls accounts prepared annually by sheriffs for the King

plantation castle castles built in Ireland on land given to those who would support the Crown

portcullis wood and iron grille-pattern gate, raised and lowered at an entrance

postern small gateway, usually at the side or rear of a castle

quatrefoil four-lobed, **six-foil** six-lobed; **trefoil** three-lobed

quoin dressed corner stone at an angle of a building

relieving arch arch built in a wall to relieve the thrust on another opening

revet face with a layer of stone for more strength. Some earth mottes were revetted with stone

rib vaulting arched roof with ribs of raised moulding at the **groins** (junction of two curved surfaces)

rubble uncut or only roughly shaped stone, for walling

scarp inner wall or slope of a ditch or moat (**counterscarp** outer wall or slope)

slight to damage or destroy a castle to render it unfit for use

solar lord's parlour or private quarters

stepped recessed in a series of ledges

stronghouse a mansion capable of being defended

turret small tower

wall-walk path along the top of a wall protected by a parapet

wing wall wall descending the slope of a motte

yett iron gates protecting an entrance

Useful Addresses & Websites

Readers may find the following organizations of use when planning a visit to any of the castles featured in this book. It is advisable to check the opening times and admission prices with the relevant body, or with the castle directly, before setting out.

ENGLAND

English Heritage
Customer Services
PO Box 569
Swindon
SN2 2YP
Customer services
tel 0870 333 1181
Membership enquiries
tel: 0870 333 1182
www.english-heritage.org.uk
Regional offices are listed on the website

The National Trust
36 Queen Anne's Gate
London
SW1H 9AS
tel: 0870 609 5380
www.nationaltrust.org.uk
Regional offices are listed on the website

SCOTLAND

Historic Scotland
Longmore House
Salisbury Place
Edinburgh
EH9 1SH
tel: 0131 668 8600
www.historic-scotland.gov.uk

The National Trust for Scotland
Wemyss House
28 Charlotte Square
Edinburgh
EH2 4ET
tel: 0131 243 9300
www.nts.org.uk

RELATED WEBSITES

www.visitscotland.com
www.scotland.com
www.travelscotland.co.uk
www.electricscotland.com
www.castlexplorer.co.uk
www.castles-of-britain.com
www.castleuk.net
www.undiscoveredscotland.co.uk
www.scottishhistory.com
www.scotshistoryonline.co.uk

The publisher can accept no responsibility for any material on external websites

Index

Note: page numbers in bold refer to maps and photographs.